The Rewards
of
SIMPLICITY

The Rewards
of
SIMPLICITY

A Practical *and Spiritual* Approach

Pam & Chuck D. Pierce

Chosen
a division of Baker Publishing Group
Grand Rapids, Michigan

© 2010 by Pam and Chuck D. Pierce

Published by Chosen Books
a division of Baker Publishing Group
P.O. Box 6287, Grand Rapids, MI 49516-6287
www.chosenbooks.com

Printed in the United States of America

Library of Congress Cataloging-in-Publication Data
Pierce, Pam.
    The rewards of simplicity : a practical and spiritual approach / Pam & Chuck D. Pierce.
        p.   cm.
    Includes bibliographical references.
    ISBN 978-0-8007-9477-4 (pbk.)
    1. Simplicity—Religious aspects—Christianity. I. Pierce, Chuck D., 1953– II. Title.
BV4647.S48P54 2010
241'.4—dc22   2009032498

Unless otherwise indicated, Scripture is taken from the New King James Version. Copyright © 1982 by Thomas Nelson, Inc. Used by permission. All rights reserved.

Scripture marked AMP is taken from the Amplified ® Bible, copyright © 1954, 1958, 1962, 1964, 1965, 1987 by The Lockman Foundation. Used by permission.

Scripture marked CJB is taken from the *Complete Jewish Bible*, copyright © 1998 by David H. Stern. Published by Jewish New Testament Publications, Inc., www.messianicjewish.net/jntp. Distributed by Messianic Jewish Resources. www.messianicjewish.net. All rights reserved. Used by permission.

Scripture marked KJV is taken from the King James Version of the Bible.

Scripture marked NIV is taken from the HOLY BIBLE, NEW INTERNATIONAL VERSION®. NIV®. Copyright © 1973, 1978, 1984 by International Bible Society. Used by permission of Zondervan. All rights reserved.

Scripture marked NLT is taken from the *Holy Bible*, New Living Translation, copyright © 1996, 2004. Used by permission of Tyndale House Publishers, Inc., Wheaton, IL 60189. All rights reserved.

10   11   12   13   14   15   16   7   6   5   4   3   2   1

This book is dedicated to our grandchildren—Hannah, Haley, Stephen, Benjamin, Chloe, Lily and Samuel—seven reasons why we choose to simplify our lives.

We love you,

Grandma and Grandpa

Contents

Introduction

Simplify. One morning last spring, I awoke from a dream with the word *simplify* ringing in my ears and in my spirit. At first, I was not completely sure if I was hearing *simplify* or *semper fi*, the U.S. Marine Corps motto. After my first cup of coffee, though, I was certain—God was clearly saying the word *simplify*.

Over the next several weeks, I sought the Lord concerning this word. I even prepared a message about simplification and shared it with my home church in Denton, Texas. Before I could begin to take my own advice about the word *simplify*, however, life—as we know it—interrupted me in all its varied and wonderful ways: the birth of a new grandchild, a conflicted teenager, children and youth summer camps, summer drama troupe and grandmotherly duties. From every corner of my house, the stacks of stuff and unattended responsibilities mocked me. All I could say in response was, "Your time is coming."

As time and a busy summer schedule permitted, I started collecting notes, ideas and information about the concept of simplification. I looked at other books dealing with the whys and hows of simplifying, some by authors much more qualified than I am. At one point, I determined that everything that needs to be said about the subject of simplification had already been said, so I set this project aside.

Then I went with my family one day to see the Pixar/Disney movie WALL•E. (Even if you are not concerned about the future of the planet, this movie is worth the time on so many levels.) Interspersed with film clips from Hello, Dolly!, WALL•E's images of a planet overrun with garbage and of a tiny robot waging war against the refuse were alternately disturbing and heartwarming. I laughed, I cried and I took a personal field trip to the local landfill.

The population of the United States alone generated 409 million tons of nonhazardous waste in municipal landfills in 2001. This total does not include waste that people dispose of in unauthorized landfills or incinerators. We Americans are filling up the landscape with garbage and throwaway consumer items at an alarming rate. Gone are the days when we could purchase a coffeepot and expect it to last for twenty years. My latest coffeemaker only made it two years, and it was a high-end model!

But what does the landfill have to do with simplification? For me, my visit to the landfill opened my eyes to a spiritual truth linked directly to our consumer lifestyle: "For what profit is it to a man if he gains the whole world, and loses his own soul?" (Matthew 16:26). If my own personal landfill is filled with cheap, broken substitutes for the real treasures available to every believer, then I obviously need to begin a serious reclamation project! Worldly substitutes for spiritual treasures never last, so like the little WALL•E robot, we need to wage war against the waste. We need to reclaim the simple, practical values that make our lives truly rewarding.

I recently revisited that morning when the Lord first spoke the word *simplify* to my groggy, pre-coffee mind. In retrospect, it was no accident that the Marine Corps motto so closely echoes what God was saying. After all, the Latin words *semper fidelis* translate into "always faithful." I believe that God, in His constant faithfulness toward His children, is calling us to simplify on every level of life so that we can clearly see the path before us.

The complications—both physical and spiritual—that clutter our modern lives are a serious threat to our communion with the Father and our relationships with our family, our friends and the rest of the world. Paul's warning to the believers in Corinth applies to us, as well: "But I fear, lest somehow, as the serpent deceived Eve by his craftiness, so your minds may be corrupted from the *simplicity* that is in Christ" (2 Corinthians 11:3, emphasis added).

So why clutter the world with another book on simplification? Good question! Simplicity is one of the spiritual disciplines practiced by Christians all over the world for the last twenty centuries. Just like prayer, meditation and fasting, simplicity holds an essential place in the life of any sincere believer seeking a deeper, more intimate communion with the Father. Many books on the market address the problems of a consumer lifestyle, for example *Affluenza* by De Graaf, Wann, and Naylor (Berrett-Koehler, 2005). Many books also address the role of simplicity as a Christian discipline, for example Richard Foster's *Celebration of Discipline* (Hodder and Stoughton, 1984). And information abounds on how to simplify one's home—just try a Google search for the word *simplify*! However, I was unable to find a book that addressed what God was saying to me about simplification. Sharing that is our goal.

I say "our" because my husband, Dr. Chuck D. Pierce, is joining me to write this book. We have come to the conclusion that to *simplify* involves much more than cleaning out closets and clearing the calendar. As we discussed this call to simplification over breakfast—the simplest, quietest part of the day in our house—we recognized that anxiety is one of its primary adversaries. Because Chuck is intimately acquainted with the enemy's use of anxiety in the believer's life, he will address that issue. Chuck's chapters in part 2 will expose the true nature of anxiety and outline some strategies for overcoming it. Anxiety wars against the call to simplify, so it is essential that we gain victory over this adversary.

As I wrote the chapters in part 1 of this book, I actively practiced what I was preaching. I wanted to maneuver my home and my life through the muddy waters of clutter into the land of simplicity—not just because it is smart or practical, but because it is what the Father requires. As we come into agreement with the Father's definition of simplification, by faith we will reap its rewards. By understanding and operating in simplicity, we open up avenues for experiencing the Holy Spirit in a whole new way. We make room for the eternal.

I invite you to join me!

Pam Pierce

PART 1

Pam Speaks on Practical and Spiritual SIMPLICITY

1

Faith, Focus and Function

One of my favorite books is C. S. Lewis's *The Lion, the Witch and the Wardrobe*. (If you have not read it, go ahead and add it to your list of "1,000 Books to Read before I Die"!) In this classic story, four children—Peter, Susan, Edmund and Lucy Pevensie—are sent to the English countryside to live with an elderly professor during World War II. Although they are unhappy about leaving their parents back in London, they determine to make the best of the situation by exploring the spacious house and the surrounding woods.

Within the first few days, Lucy discovers an entrance to another world—Narnia—through an old wardrobe in the spare room. Her siblings do not believe her, but soon her brother Edmund finds his way into Narnia on his own. Shortly after this (and I am definitely giving you the abridged version of the story), the children are wandering around the house while the housekeeper, Mrs. Macready, is taking visitors on a tour of the historic residence. The children try desperately to stay one step ahead of the disagreeable housekeeper. C. S.

Lewis writes, "And after that—whether it was that they lost their heads, or that Mrs. Macready was trying to catch them, or that some magic in the house had come to life and was chasing them into Narnia—they seemed to find themselves being followed everywhere."[1]

And so, the children find themselves being guided by an unseen hand into the spare room containing the wardrobe. When the spare room doorknob rattles, the children clamber inside the wardrobe, only to tumble out on the other side into Narnia.

Like the four Pevensie children, we are often guided by an unseen Hand into places that force us to experience a new dimension of faith. Our Father is faithful, and we can trust Him to lead us into the right pastures at the right times, regardless of the circumstances. For many of us, a call to simplify is a new pasture that requires us to trust and obey the Lord in new ways.

I have discovered three essential keys, or perspectives, to unlocking simplicity in our lives. Every aspect of simplicity can be viewed from these three perspectives: faith, focus and function. When we attempt to achieve simplification in any area of our lives without these three perspectives, we are in danger of falling into legalism. These keys are the subject of this chapter. But first, let me share just one example of how the Lord maneuvers us into difficult places for His wonderful purposes.

Christmas Flood

Boy's Country, a children's home in southeast Texas, had provided us a lovely little house when my husband, Chuck, joined the staff in 1983. After a few months as temporary houseparents in one of the group cottages, we moved back into the staff house in time to decorate for Christmas. Stockings hung over the fireplace, a small tree stood in the front window and a modest assortment of gifts anchored the tree to the floor.

The week before Christmas, a flock of Canadian geese landed in the cornfield next to our house. We watched in fascination as the bare field, dotted with the skeletal remains of corn, turned into a sea of honking, gray and white birds. Within hours of the birds' arrival, an arctic front dipped into our area, plunging us into the coldest December I could remember.

On Christmas Day, in spite of the nose-numbing cold, we drove into Houston to spend the day with friends. After a festive day of food and fellowship, we loaded up all the goodies and returned to Boy's Country. The geese stirred themselves when the car's headlights illuminated the cornfield. They honked in protest, but they settled back to sleep as we approached the front door.

We knew something was wrong as soon as we stepped onto the front porch. The concrete was wet, and water was seeping out from under the front door. Chuck and I looked at each other with dread as he opened the door. Within seconds, our feet were soaked with the cold water pouring out of the house. The pipes in the attic had frozen, then burst, and we had not been there to turn off the water! After wading down the hallway, we discovered the source of the flood. The ceiling over our bed had collapsed, releasing a cold waterfall into the bedroom. *Merry Christmas.*

The next several hours are a merciful blur in my memory. Chuck claims that I conveniently forget unpleasant details, and he is right. It works for me. Regardless of my coping mechanisms, we did manage to get the water turned off and found enough dry clothing and essentials to set up in one of

17

the vacant group cottages. The boys and the houseparents were gone during the Christmas break, so we had a huge kitchen and four rooms of bunk beds to choose from while our staff house was put back together.

You may be wondering what all this has to do with simplicity. At the time, all I could see was the mess. As I slogged through the flooded staff house in search of the few things I would really need for the next couple of weeks, I wondered what possible purpose a flooded house could serve.

It is amazing how little we actually need, materially speaking, to live. During the time the flood forced us out of our house, God provided a warm, comfortable place for us to live. Granted, it was not "our" place, but we were grateful for it! The only things we brought with us to the group cottage were clothes and toiletries, some of two-year-old Daniel's favorite toys and books, our Bibles, more books and our personal journals. Our weather-related circumstances had herded us into a temporarily simpler way of life.

We all know that hindsight is 20/20, and it did not take us long to look back and see what God had ordained for us during our displacement. First, during the chilly, early morning hours when sleeping in a bunk bed was impossible for Chuck, God began to give my husband revelation of things to come. In his other books, Chuck has shared what the Lord showed him about the dissolution of communism in the Soviet Union and political shifts around the world. Suffice it to say that God eliminated the distraction of routine and comfort to speak to my husband with more clarity than Chuck had ever experienced before.

By early January, it became apparent that we would not be moving back into our staff house for at least another week. Christmas break was quickly coming to an end, and the boys would soon be back in their own bunk beds. We would have to find another place to stay for a few more days.

Once again, God started leading. This time, He led us north, to Denton, Texas. As we drove to church that Sunday, a white panel truck pulled out in front of us. The truck was covered with a thick layer of dirt in which someone had written "Follow me." When we pulled up closer to the truck, we saw the name of a plant and feed company located in Denton, Texas.

"That's interesting," I commented.

"Why is it interesting?" Chuck wanted to know.

"The book I just finished reading is dedicated to an organization that's based in Denton."

"What's the organization?"

"Mission: Possible," I said. "They provide Bibles, materials and other forms of assistance to the Church behind the Iron Curtain."

Chuck was thoughtful. I knew he was thinking about what the Lord had been speaking to him lately concerning the Soviet Union and changes that would soon occur in the communist bloc.

"That *is* interesting," he agreed. And with that, it was settled: We would go to Denton.

Chuck has shared much of this testimony in other places, but I want to approach it from the perspective of faith and simplicity. First of all, we do not consider every dirty truck with the words "Follow me" written in the grime to be a word from God. I normally consider that to be a sign that someone needs to take a ride through the car wash. Even so, God can and does use ordinary things like a dirty panel truck to direct His people.

Of course, the fact that Chuck's family lived in the Denton area meant that we would have a place to stay for a few days. So we packed a suitcase, buckled Daniel into his car seat and headed north. And on that trip, I discovered the first—and most important—key to simplicity.

The First Key: Faith

In Hebrews 11:6, we read the following: "But without faith it is impossible to please Him, for he who comes to God must believe that He is, and that He is a rewarder of those who diligently seek Him."

Faith is the starting place for every vital pursuit in the Christian life, for without it we can never hope to please God. From the moment we first believe, faith is the essential element. Our knowledge of the Lord Jesus Christ, our agreement with His Word and the diligent application of His will in our lives begins with faith and brings us into new and precious places of communion with the Father. And so, faith is the obvious starting place for us if we truly desire simplicity.

As I said at the start, Christians everywhere have practiced simplicity as a spiritual discipline for twenty centuries. Simplicity is never meant to become legalistic drudgery, though, nor should any of the other spiritual disciplines such as prayer, meditation and fasting become so. Instead, they are meant to be freeing and fulfilling. Internal simplicity will result in external freedom.

How do we approach the spiritual discipline of simplicity by faith? Like so many other situations in our lives, sometimes the Lord uses what we consider to be unfortunate—even uncomfortable—events to steer us into His will and His ways.

Somewhere along that five-hour trip to North Texas, Chuck and I began discussing the issue of raising hands in worship. At that time in our lives, we were members of a traditional, evangelical church in northwest Houston. Our worship services were orderly, frequently moving, dotted with the occasional "amen," but never disrupted by someone raising his or her hands in worship. That is, until Chuck came along and started rocking the boat! For some reason, I chose this ride in the car to tell my husband how embarrassing it was for me when he stood up and raised his hands in church.

"I mean, really, Chuck," I said, "is it necessary? Hand raising is only mentioned in the Bible a few times."

"It wouldn't matter to me if hand raising were only mentioned one time in the Bible," Chuck explained. "That would be enough for me. And it's more important to me that I obey the Lord when I worship than to worry about whether you are comfortable with it."

The next several miles were quiet in the car. I knew he was right, but I did not want to admit that physical demonstrations of worship and adoration were difficult for me. If I were honest, I would admit that I envied Chuck's ability to worship with such abandon. But I was not that honest—yet.

Once we arrived in Denton, Chuck remembered that James Robison would be hosting his Bible conference that same week in Dallas. We left Daniel with his grandmother and drove to Reunion Arena for the meeting that changed my life.

Chuck and I had adopted our two-year-old, Daniel, after eight years of marriage. I had been told by two doctors that, without surgery, I would be unable to conceive a child naturally. I had chosen not to have the surgery, but I had continued to seek the Lord for supernatural healing. That day in Dallas, I raised my hands in worship for the first time in my life. I will never forget how liberated I felt. I finally understood what Chuck had already discovered. My simple act of obedience opened a window over me that allowed the healing power of God to pour over my body like warm honey. In that instant, God sovereignly healed me of barrenness. By February, I was pregnant for the first time in my life. Through a Christmas flood, God had steered me to the right place at the right time so that I could receive healing by faith.

Simplicity strips away those things in our lives that clutter, hinder and obstruct our vision. By faith, we can enter into a new dimension of simplicity, the kind of simplicity that clears out the heart as well as the closet. By faith, we can focus on those people, activities and ideas that matter to us—and to the Lord Jesus Christ—the most.

The Second Key: Focus

After faith, the second key to unlocking simplicity is focus. Focus is the ability to narrow our vision and concentrate on the moment instead of all the peripheral concerns that strive for our attention. Many years after that day in Dallas, one of my children demonstrated the power of focus when he wanted to learn something new.

The summer of 2000 was one of the hottest—and driest— in recent Texas history. Our family had just moved back to North Texas after a two-year sojourn in Colorado Springs. While some would have considered that time a vacation, it was more like an exile for me. I am a native Texan, and in spite of the long, hot summers, the insects and the occasional snake in the garden, I love my home state. So two years in a place with long, cold winters and virtually no summer were enough for me!

We moved into a house with just enough room for our family and settled into our routine in time to start homeschooling again in late August. Daniel, my eighteen-year-old, had graduated from high school in Colorado that spring and moved back to Texas the next week. That left four children at home to educate: Ethan, Isaac, John Mark and Rebekah. As the oldest son in the house, John Mark immediately laid claim to the small bedroom right next to the kitchen so he would not have to share a room with his two younger brothers. Within a few weeks, we would all be grateful for his choice.

John Mark had developed an interest in the guitar before we moved back to Texas but had not made much progress. Not long after we returned home, he started meeting with another young man in our church once a week for lessons. Micah was a gifted musician and a patient teacher who would later become one of John Mark's best friends. Every week, Micah would teach his student new chords and skills, and John Mark would return home to practice. And practice. And practice.

Three weeks into guitar lessons, the whole family was thankful that a kitchen, living room and hallway separated John Mark's bedroom from the rest of the house. He practiced every spare minute. In fact, he practiced during most minutes. Homeschooling was "on hold" while John Mark practiced. At the age of fourteen, my son had determined to learn to play the guitar, and if that meant he had to practice ten hours a day, then that is what he would do. It almost drove us crazy.

One night I walked into John Mark's room after midnight to turn off the light. He had fallen asleep practicing chords, and the guitar was lying beside the bed. As I propped the instrument against the desk, I noticed that John Mark's left hand was moving: He was forming chords in his sleep.

My son's single-minded determination to learn something new is an excellent illustration of what it means to simplify. Researching the dictionary definition of the word *simplify*, I found the following list:

- To make simple or simpler
- To reduce to basic essentials

- To diminish in scope or complexity—streamline
- To make more intelligible—clarify[2]

When John Mark determined to play the guitar, he unconsciously followed these definitions of *simplify*. First, he reduced the complexity of his life. Obviously, a homeschooling fourteen-year-old boy does not have a lot of responsibilities to start with, but the ones he did have took a backseat! Next, he reduced the task at hand into its fundamental parts by taking it one new skill at a time. He mastered one chord at a time before moving forward. Of course, that meant the entire household got an earful of the G chord before he finally moved on to another chord, but we all understood John's need for focus. And finally, John Mark reached the point in his learning where he understood how all the parts of playing the guitar fit together as a whole. From that point on, John was able to shift his focus from individual skills to technique and style. And for the rest of the household, that meant more hours of quiet throughout the day!

John Mark focused on his goal and eliminated every obstacle in his path toward success. While part of my son's success can be traced back to his personal character and temperament, there is no mistaking the role that simplicity played—and continues to play—in his life.

In the book of James, we read the following admonition concerning godly focus: "But when he asks, he must believe and not doubt, because he who doubts is like a wave of the sea, blown and tossed by the wind. That man should not think he will receive anything from the Lord; he is a double-minded man, unstable in all he does" (James 1:6–8, NIV).

I realize that in our efforts to simplify, not all of us are blessed with the flexible schedule of a fourteen-year-old homeschooler. John Mark was in a unique position at that time to narrow his focus on learning guitar while excluding other things. There is also something to be said, though, about approaching things with the single-minded determination of the young. Along with the faith of a child, perhaps we should pay closer attention to the focus of a child.

The Third Key: Function

Back in 1983, when Chuck and I lived at Boy's Country in southeast Texas, God had orchestrated circumstances in our lives to maneuver us into a temporary place of simplicity. At the time, we were not aware that we were operating in the spiritual discipline of simplicity; we just knew that God had momentarily stripped us down to the bare necessities so that He could bless us. Simplicity is a place of blessing for believers, whether we enter into it by accident or design. When we move by faith, with focus, into the function of simplicity, blessings abound!

The book of James is a refreshingly straightforward look at the Christian life. James bluntly and honestly lays down the basics concerning the life of faith. In chapter two, we read the following:

> But someone will say, "You have faith, and I have works." Show me your faith without your works, and I will show you my faith by my works. You believe that there is one God. You do well. Even the demons believe—and tremble! But do you want to know, O foolish man, that faith without works is dead? Was not Abraham our father justified by works when he offered Isaac his son on the altar? Do you see that faith was working together with his works, and by works faith was made perfect? And the Scripture was fulfilled which says, "Abraham believed God, and it was accounted to him for righteousness." And he was called the friend of

God. You see then that a man is justified by works, and not by faith only.

Likewise, was not Rahab the harlot also justified by works when she received the messengers and sent them out another way?

For as the body without the spirit is dead, so faith without works is dead also.

James 2:18–26

If faith is the starting place for a simplified life, and focus aligns our hearts and minds to God's purposes, then function is the evidence of simplicity in the believer's life. Faith demonstrates its viability through works. Oswald Chambers, the nineteenth-century evangelical minister from Scotland, said this about simplicity in his book *The Servant as His Lord*: "The marvel of the grace of God is that He can take the strands of evil and twistedness out of a man's mind and imagination and make him simple towards God. Restoration through the Redemption of Jesus Christ makes a man simple, and simplicity always shows itself in action."[3]

When Oswald Chambers penned these words, I do not believe he was thinking about cleaning out his closets and reorganizing the kitchen. Instead, he was referring to the renewed mind of the believer being free to understand the mysteries of faith, focus on the Savior and function efficiently in a chaotic, fallen world. All kinds of freedom flow out of the renewed mind! In fact, according to the book of Romans, the renewed mind is the key to discerning the will of God:

Therefore, I urge you, brothers, in view of God's mercy, to offer your bodies as living sacrifices, holy and pleasing to God—this is your spiritual act of worship. Do not conform any longer to the pattern of this world, but be transformed by the renewing of your mind. Then you will be able to test and approve what God's will is—his good, pleasing and perfect will.

Romans 12:1–2, NIV

True simplicity flows out of a renewed mind and changes worldly patterns that result in confusion. Simplicity is sparked by faith and inevitably manifests itself in our lives in tangible, visible ways. It is impossible to experience inner, spiritual simplicity without the accompanying outer, physical simplification. Like faith, simplicity reveals itself through works, exposing the beauty of the Savior in the process. Function, then, is the practical application of faith and focus in the believer's life as it relates to the spiritual discipline of simplicity. By the power of the Holy Spirit working in our hearts, simplicity works its way from the inside out and creates an uncluttered atmosphere.

Choosing the Good Part

When it comes to simplification, getting the cart before the horse is a real danger. Many of us want—even need—to plunge headlong into "doing" when we really need to focus on "being" first! That is why it is so important to start the discipline of simplicity with faith and narrow our focus before moving on to the function.

Martha and Mary, the sisters of Lazarus, illustrate this concept in the New Testament. Let's look at these two women's lives through the eyes of Someone who knew them well. In Luke 10:38, we meet Martha for the first time. According to this verse, Martha invites Jesus into her house. If we read between the lines, it is apparent that Martha presides over her household with pride and efficiency. Mary, who lives with her sister, is obviously more interested in their visitor than she is in fixing dinner:

27

Now it happened as they went that He entered a certain village; and a certain woman named Martha welcomed Him into her house. And she had a sister called Mary, who also sat at Jesus' feet and heard His word. But Martha was distracted with much serving, and she approached Him and said, "Lord, do You not care that my sister has left me to serve alone? Therefore tell her to help me."

And Jesus answered and said to her, "Martha, Martha, you are worried and troubled about many things. But one thing is needed, and Mary has chosen that good part, which will not be taken away from her."

Luke 10:38–42

Over the years, I have heard countless sermons and Bible lessons about Mary, Martha and their encounter with Jesus. I believe we can benefit from a closer examination of this encounter. (Personally, I think Martha receives a lot of criticism based on this one incident. After all, not long after this, Martha demonstrates her faith and understanding when she tells Jesus in John 11:21–22, "Lord, if You had been here, my brother would not have died. But even now I know that whatever You ask of God, God will give You." But that is another story!)

Martha is a homemaker, and she takes her responsibilities seriously. When she invites a guest into her home for a meal and fellowship, she is focused on serving. Her desire is that her guest knows he is welcome, honored and cared for. That is all good. In fact, that is part of the gift of hospitality. The problem is that Martha expects Mary, who operates from a different mindset, to join her in the kitchen and help with meal preparations. In some circumstances, that would be the right thing for Mary to do. However, this time, if Mary goes to the kitchen out of a sense of duty, she will miss a precious time of fellowship with Jesus.

When Martha goes to Jesus with her complaint, she plays the part of the petulant sibling appealing to a parent. Those of us who have experienced the joys (and trials!) of growing up with brothers or sisters recognize the scenario unfolding in Martha's house. Martha is doing all the work while Mary has all the fun! Rather than set the work aside and join her sister at Jesus' feet, Martha wants Jesus to acknowledge her service and deny Mary the "good part" she has chosen.

As members of spiritual and physical families, it is essential for us to recognize and appreciate our differences. Some of us are motivated by serving others. Some of us are motivated by sitting at the feet of Jesus. All of us have to learn, as Martha did, that choosing the "good part" sometimes involves letting go of what seems important so that we can enjoy what is truly important. Based on Martha's declaration to Jesus later, after the death of Lazarus, I believe we can conclude that Martha learned how to simplify her household routine when Jesus came to visit! Otherwise, she would not have had time to know Him as the Christ.

The "Martha Syndrome" is not limited to women running households. On the contrary, men are just as susceptible to this malady! All of us are in danger of being "worried and troubled about many things." Whether we are worried about job security, the environment, our children, our friends, our health, terrorism or the house payment, there always seems to be enough trouble to go around! That is why it is so important that we learn to choose that good part.

Using the Keys

A key is useless until we insert it into a lock, turn it and open the door. We must use the key of faith to unlock the door to simplicity. Then, with our focus on Jesus, we can function in the world with new clarity.

As I write this chapter, it is January 2009. It seems as though every magazine in the grocery store is focused on starting the new year with an organized house and life. *Better Homes and Gardens* announces "45 Smart Ways to Cure Clutter Forever." *Family Circle* encourages readers to "Get Organized: 101 Simple (& Cheap) Ideas." And *Real Simple* says "Feel Calmer Now: 20 Essential Lists to Organize Your Life." These and many other publications hit the newsstand every January and offer advice for simplifying, organizing and improving our lives by arranging the externals in more manageable segments!

In this book, we propose a different approach. Our purpose is to present spiritual and practical frameworks for the Christian discipline of simplicity, based on the Word of God and our own experiences. While it is wise to receive counsel and instruction from others, including organizational experts, the function of simplicity must begin with attention to our inner selves. No matter how uncluttered, organized and simplified our façade may appear, it is the heart that counts. In subsequent chapters, we will clarify and—dare I suggest?—*simplify* the spiritual discipline of simplicity from several perspectives.

2

Understanding Simplicity

In chapter 1, I explained that the definition of the word *simplify* includes making simpler, reducing to basic essentials, streamlining and making more intelligible by clarifying. When we follow the definition back a little further, we discover that the word *simple* means "having or composed of only one thing, element, or part; not involved or complicated; being without additions or modifications; having little or no ornamentation; not embellished or adorned."[1]

In other words, if something is simple, it is unpretentious, free of guile and undefiled. Simplicity, then, is the state of being simple, clear and free of affectation. That, indeed, is an excellent state of being for the believer!

While we ponder the beauty of simplicity, let me share a story with you about what it means to be simple. When I was ten years old, my family moved from Southern California to Lake Jackson, Texas. My parents, my sister and I loaded all of our essential belongings into an unair-conditioned car and headed east early in the spring of 1964. Along the way, we stopped in Arizona for a quick look at the Grand Canyon. Even though we only walked to the edge and looked over the rim of the canyon, the hugeness of the place made a tremendous impression on my young mind. Ever since, I have promised myself that I would return one day and do more than look over the edge.

In October 2008, I kept that promise. After months of planning, I headed west with six other passengers: my friend Susan; my daughter, Rebekah, and her husband, Nathan; my youngest sons, Isaac and Ethan, and their friend Bryan. We loaded up the van and left Denton, Texas, on a beautiful fall morning. After stopping overnight in Albuquerque—where we ate some delicious Mexican food—we completed the journey across Arizona the next day. By the time we reached our motel just outside the entrance to Grand Canyon National Park, it was too dark to go to the canyon. We settled in for another night of waiting.

The next morning dawned clear and cool. I was so eager to reach our destination that I could barely eat breakfast! As soon as everyone was finished eating, showering and packing, we loaded into the van for the last few miles. The car was pulsating with anticipation. When we finally reached the entrance to the park, we were absolutely giddy with excitement. At Mather Point, the first observation area beyond the entrance, I parked the van and took a deep breath.

"Everybody listen!" my daughter, Rebekah, commanded before we opened the van doors. "Keep your eyes on the pavement until we get to the edge. Then we'll all look into the canyon at the same time."

For just a moment, I was actually afraid that we had allowed our excitement and anticipation to set us up for disappointment. *What if that first glimpse isn't what we expect?* I thought. *Surely that won't be the case!* And it certainly was not.

I had read that people have many different reactions when they first step to the rim of the Grand Canyon and look into the chasm. Some people cry, others laugh uncontrollably and others are overcome with vertigo. For me, that moment when we all reached the edge together and looked out was emotional, physical and spiritual. Emotionally, I was overcome with the realization that I had finally made it back to a place that figured so prominently in my tumultuous childhood. Physically, I experienced a visceral response deep in my chest every time I looked over the rim. Spiritually, I was overwhelmed with gratitude to the Father for giving such a breathtaking gift to His children.

For the next several days, we walked, climbed and explored as much of the South Rim of the Grand Canyon as we could. We were amazed at how the canyon presented so many different perspectives of itself, depending on where and when one stood and looked. We were also reminded of the limits of our lungs when we ventured down Bright Angel Trail! Going down is one thing; climbing back up is quite another!

On the last night of our Grand Canyon adventure, we returned to Yavapai Point to watch the sun set. While we were waiting, we ventured inside the observation station to look at the exhibits and gift shop. On the wall, just above a sign that said "Standing on the Shoulders of Giants," I read these words:

> This chasm has been studied and restudied by generations of geologists. For as grandly simple as this place appears . . . we continue to be presented with new facts, new interpretations, and new lessons.
>
> Earle Spamer

Grandly simple. Seems like an oxymoron, yet as I stood on the canyon's edge for one last sunset, I understood what it

33

meant. The Grand Canyon needs no embellishment or ornamentation. It is simply grand. The geologic layers exposed
by the Colorado River are beautifully varied and mysterious.
Further study and exploration only serve to increase our ap-
preciation of the canyon.

In the same way, when a believer enters into the discipline
of simplicity, he will discover beautifully varied and mysterious layers in his own life. Let's dig a little deeper and uncover
some of those layers for ourselves.

Circumspect Simplicity

As is the case with any discipline, we must approach simplicity deliberately. In Ephesians, the apostle Paul instructs
the church regarding careful living: "See then that you walk
circumspectly, not as fools but as wise, redeeming the time,
because the days are evil. Therefore do not be unwise, but
understand what the will of the Lord is" (5:15–17). This
passage can be applied to every aspect of life, no matter how
lofty or mundane, but it is essential to our understanding of
the concept of simplicity.

The word *circumspect* is defined as "heedful of circumstances and potential consequences; prudent."[2] The Latin
prefix *circum* means "around" or "about," as in a circle, and
the suffix, *spek* means "to watch" or "to look at." The first
time I read Ephesians 5:15 with understanding, it was because
I was able to visualize what the apostle had in mind when he
said to "walk circumspectly." Clearly, walking circumspectly
involves examining our options and opportunities from all
angles so that we see the circumstances and possible out-
comes. When we walk circumspectly in regard to simplicity,
we respond with godly wisdom to the complications inherent in our lives. This means we walk around a situation and

look at it carefully before committing to action. We do not rush in like fools, but rather, we "understand what the will of the Lord is."

As I have said before, simplicity is more than cleaning out closets and reducing the amount of time we waste on frivolous activity. Simplicity, when approached from a mindset of faith, involves walking around the perimeter of activities, options, commitments, even relationships, and examining them with an eye of wisdom. Because we are limited beings endowed with purpose, it is vital that we eliminate those things that are contrary to the will of the Lord. We must learn to prune away those things that hinder our divine purpose and embrace those things that are needful.

It is important to remember that simplicity will vary from one person to the next. In fact, it will vary from one family member to another! I cannot "walk circumspectly" around my husband's options and opportunities and assume that I know how he should simplify his life, nor can he presume to do the same for me. Let me share an example of what I mean.

Simplified Gardening

I am a gardener. Two years ago, I spent 140 hours becoming a certified Texas Master Gardener by completing 70 hours of training and 70 hours of service in Denton County, Texas. Because this was important to me, I adjusted my other obligations and responsibilities to accommodate my training and service. I had to evaluate my schedule, simplify my daily routine and budget my time in a whole new way. By the end of 2007, I had accomplished my goal: I was certified!

Last fall, I was cleaning out flower beds and preparing my vegetable garden for winter. My husband, Chuck, followed me outside after one of my water breaks.

"So," he began, surveying the piles ready for composting, "why don't you simplify your garden for next year?"

"What?" I asked, incredulous. "What exactly does that mean?"

"Well, it just seems so complicated."

I stood up, pruners in hand, to face my non-gardening husband.

"Chuck, do you know what the oldest profession is?" I asked.

"Is that a trick question?" he responded, eyeing the pruners.

"No, it's not a trick question," I continued. "The oldest profession is gardening. God is a gardener, and He put Adam and Eve to work *in the Garden of Eden.*"

"Okay," he conceded. "But wouldn't your life be easier if you had a simpler garden? I mean, if God is saying to simplify, it would make sense to apply that principle to your gardening."

I am sure that, to Chuck, this made sense. To him, gardening and yard work consumed a lot of my "leisure time," especially during the growing season. I knew I would have to formulate my answer carefully.

"Honey, I love working out here, even in the heat of the summer," I began. "The only thing I don't like about gardening is waiting for winter to pass so that I can get out and garden again! So, if I'm going to simplify something in my life by eliminating or reducing it, then I'll eliminate or reduce housework and laundry! Unless God puts His finger on gardening and tells me to change something, I'll keep on digging, okay?"

I enjoy every aspect of gardening, from soil preparation to pulling weeds. I understand that every step is important, and there are no shortcuts to a healthy, productive garden.

And, while Chuck enjoys the finished products of my labor (that is, flowers and fruit!), he does not want me to work too hard or get heatstroke in the Texas summer. So I understand his motivation for wanting me to simplify my garden, but if simplification involves skipping important tasks in the yard, it will only result in more work in the end.

When we share our lives with others, we have to consider their passions and preferences before trying to help them simplify their lives. Even though I do not share Chuck's enthusiasm about bowling, I would not dream of asking him to give it up for the sake of simplicity. For Chuck, bowling provides a welcome respite from the responsibilities of a busy ministry. Like gardening for me, bowling with his league buddies is a pleasure for Chuck, not a chore. Besides, when Chuck is bowling, I can dig!

The purpose of simplicity is not to prune away those things that bring us joy and enrich our lives. Instead, the purpose of simplicity is to streamline our lives in such a way that we have more room, time and energy for the pursuits and people that God ordains for us. This kind of simplification will require circumspection and wisdom from the Father.

We often confuse *simple* with *easy*. Although we do find the two words listed as synonyms, the concept of simplicity is anything but easy when we start applying it to our lives. Once again, my children can help me illustrate the point.

Gifted or Skilled?

In chapter 1, I shared a story about my son John Mark and his focused determination while learning to play the guitar. Not long after the interminable practice sessions faded into memory, John Mark decided he wanted to learn how to play the drums. Consequently, for his birthday in March 2002, we bought John a set of Pearl drums. By that time, we had converted the garage into a combination classroom and hobby area, so at least the drums would not be in the main house. If learning to play the drums was anything like learning to play the guitar, I knew that it would get noisy.

Within minutes of setting up his new drum set, John Mark was diligently applying himself to the new challenge. The steady rhythm of drum and high hat filled the southwest corner of the house. I discovered that I could barely hear the drums from my bedroom, so I retreated to that part of the house whenever possible. I contemplated buying earplugs, but then remembered that I would not hear what my other children were doing if I chose that option. Ah, the things we parents suffer for our children's musical dreams!

John Mark's younger brother, twelve-year-old Isaac, had never shown any interest in playing an instrument until the drums arrived. One day not long after John's birthday, Isaac sat down at the drums with a set of sticks. What happened next still baffles me. With no instruction, Isaac started playing, tentatively at first, then with increasing dexterity. Within hours, Isaac was demonstrating unusual skill. Although John Mark continued to practice and apply himself to learning the drums, it was apparent that Isaac would be the drummer in the family. Even though John possessed the focus and determination for learning anything he wanted to learn, Isaac exposed his musical gifting when he discovered the drums.

In the realm of musical ability, John Mark and Isaac are two sides of the same coin. John Mark exhibits the characteristics of skill, while Isaac displays the results of gifting. According to the dictionary, the word *skill* is defined as "proficiency, facility, or dexterity that is acquired or developed through training or experience." The word *gift* is defined as "something bestowed voluntarily and without compensation;

a talent, endowment, aptitude or inclination," and the word *gifted* means "endowed with great natural ability, intelligence or talent."[3]

Whether Isaac is musically gifted by genetic inheritance, spiritual favor or both is not really important. What matters is that Isaac recognizes his musical ability as a gift from God to develop and exercise. John Mark's musical skill, on the other hand, flows out of his God-given focus and determination.

Eventually, Isaac discovered that being gifted musically did not mean he could skip the part requiring focus and determination. Just like his brother, he would need a teacher to help him develop his gift beyond the basics. The ease of being gifted would only take him so far; he still had to choose to prune away attitudes and mindsets that could limit his gift for the future. He, too, would have to move by *faith* and receive instruction, *focus* on the objective and learn to *function* as a drummer with other musicians.

Learning to play the drums was easy for Isaac because of his gifting. Even so, he recognizes that his ability on the drums is the result not of his labor but of the grace of God. On the flip side, John Mark recognizes that his ability on the guitar (and now, on the bass) is the result of God-given characteristics that he has chosen to develop. Both boys (now grown men) have learned the value of faith, focus and function in simplifying their lives in the area of musical development.

Recognizing our heavenly Father as the source of all we have is central to the concept of simplicity. Our gifts, temperaments, blessings and even our daily bread are the direct result of a gracious, good God who loves us and shares His abundance with us freely. When we understand that everything we have, both eternal and temporal, proceeds from His hand, then we are able to respond to His call to simplify without fear or anxiety.

Seeking the Kingdom

No discussion of simplicity would be complete without addressing the role of seeking the Kingdom. In Chuck's chapters on anxiety in part 2, he will deal with the role of faith in everyday life. Central to the life of faith is the principle of seeking the Kingdom. Nowhere in Scripture is this concept more clearly outlined than in the following passage:

> Therefore I say to you, do not worry about your life, what you will eat or what you will drink; nor about your body, what you will put on. Is not life more than food and the body more than clothing? Look at the birds of the air, for they neither sow nor reap nor gather into barns; yet your heavenly Father feeds them. Are you not of more value than they? Which of you by worrying can add one cubit to his stature?
>
> So why do you worry about clothing? Consider the lilies of the field, how they grow: they neither toil nor spin; and yet I say to you that even Solomon in all his glory was not arrayed like one of these. Now if God so clothes the grass of the field, which today is, and tomorrow is thrown into the oven, will He not much more clothe you, O you of little faith?
>
> Therefore do not worry, saying, "What shall we eat?" or "What shall we drink?" or "What shall we wear?" For after all these things the Gentiles seek. For your heavenly Father knows that you need all these things. But seek first the kingdom of God and His righteousness, and all these things shall be added to you.
>
> Matthew 6:25–33

As we will see further in Chuck's chapters on the subject, anxiety robs us of joy and hinders the Holy Spirit in the believer's life. Worry over our safety, our provision, our future keeps us bound to the earthly realm in such a way that simplicity is literally out of reach. When we choose to practice the discipline of simplicity by faith, we allow the Holy Spirit access to our cluttered minds to clear out the spiritual debris.

This concept came to life for my husband and me early in our marriage. In 1975, when Chuck graduated from Texas A&M University, he accepted a job in Houston with an energy company. For the next five years, Chuck experienced the favor of God in the workplace. He rose within the company from computer programmer to assistant director of personnel. He was, to quote one of his bosses, the "golden-haired boy" of the company.

During this same time period, we experienced a spiritual awakening in our personal lives. The Word of God came to life for us, we were baptized in the Holy Spirit and we were walking in the promises of God like never before. Everything had come together for us in such a way that anything and everything seemed possible. I had even reached a point in my own life where being childless was no longer an issue for me. After years of prayer and pain, I had submitted my life and my womb to the Father. If I was to remain childless, I was okay with that. Jesus really was enough.

So there we were, two twenty-something, career-minded, Spirit-filled Christians living a wonderful life in suburbia. Then everything changed. One day God called Chuck to the ministry. Within weeks, Chuck had resigned from a financially secure career to follow a call into full-time ministry *without pay*. For one year, Chuck worked on staff at our church in Houston without accepting a salary. The church was in the midst of building a new education building debt-free, and Chuck knew that his offering was to be a year of service as building administrator. During that year, we relied on my salary as a church secretary, our savings and the goodness of God's people to live.

At the end of that year, when the new education building was complete, our pastor asked Chuck to stay on staff with salary. Chuck agreed, and we began a new year with the prospect of additional monthly income to take care of our needs. That is, until the first check came! That is when God gave my husband new instructions: Chuck was to work another year without salary, but this time, no one was to know. Every payday, Chuck accepted his check, signed the back and put it in the offering plate.

That was an interesting year. I was still working in the church office myself. The Lord had not told me to sign my check over, but secretaries did not make a lot of money in 1980. It was not long before our savings account and energy company stock were depleted. Even so, we knew that God had set our course, and that meant He would provide.

And He did. He taught me to be creative with whatever we had in the kitchen. Granted, a few times we ate oatmeal for supper, but we actually like oatmeal! Several years before embarking on this adventure, God had led us to eliminate credit cards and live on a cash basis, so living on credit was not an option. Every time we were about to run out of food or money to pay bills, God would send just what we needed in the nick of time. We learned more about simplification in that one year than we ever imagined possible!

As I mentioned, I had submitted myself to the Lord concerning barrenness two years before this. I believed that God had children somewhere in our future, and I was willing to wait as long as necessary to receive the promise. Imagine my surprise when the promise arrived during this year of oatmeal and provision by faith! By October 1981, Chuck and I had welcomed our first child, Daniel, by private adoption, and the lawyer donated her time and services free of charge!

As that life-changing year came to a close, Chuck and I did not know what to expect next. We had learned firsthand that when we "seek first the kingdom of God and His righteousness," every need—and many precious desires—are added to our lives. By seeking the Kingdom, submitting to the discipline of simplicity and walking in faith, we allowed the Father to expose beautifully varied and mysterious layers in our lives.

A Simplification Mindset

In chapter 1, I referred briefly to the concept of the renewed mind and quoted Romans 12:1–2, which urges us to be transformed by the renewing of our minds so we can test and approve what God's will is. Simplification naturally flows out of the renewed mind and changes the way we function in the world. When we allow the Holy Spirit to renew our minds with the Word of God, we are transformed. That transformation results in a new mindset, a mindset that is aligned with God's priorities, plans and practices. We become people who operate under different parameters than the world, including the ones we have discussed in this chapter:

• We will recognize the grand simplicity in our own and other's lives.
• We will walk circumspectly, wisely, in the world.
• We will prune our own gardens without assuming we can prune someone else's!
• We will recognize the gracious provision of a loving Father and receive every gift with gratitude.

43

- We will seek first the Kingdom and trust the Father for everything else.

These internal characteristics will equip us as we put the discipline of simplification to practice in our lives. As we examine our habits and lifestyles in the rest of this book, it is important to remember why simplification is so important to the Body of Christ in this hour: "But I fear, lest somehow, as the serpent deceived Eve by his craftiness, so your minds may be corrupted from the simplicity that is in Christ" (2 Corinthians 11:3).

Let's focus on the simplicity that is in Christ Jesus.

3

Fasting for Simplification

I was born into a world on the edge of tremendous change. I have watched as the land of my childhood evolved into an unrecognizable environment. Within a few short decades, children in the United States have morphed into little adults who are technically savvy and as busy as their parents. In 1960, when I started school, we had one black-and-white console television, a radio and a record player in our home. When I came home from school in the afternoon, there were no tae kwon do lessons or soccer games to rush off to. The most pressing thing on my six-year-old agenda was how fast I could change into play clothes and get outside!

My childhood, though far from idyllic, was full of creative, outdoor play, books and neighborhoods full of friends. School was structured and demanding, and the closest thing to technology in the classroom was a filmstrip. The first time I watched television in school was when President Kennedy was assassinated in November 1963. I would not do that again until 1968.

The clutter in our lives has multiplied considerably since 1960. Demands for our time and attention bombard us from every quarter. In the midst of this bombardment, the need to simplify is even more urgent.

If you have ever read *Walden* by Henry David Thoreau, you will be familiar with this quote: "Our life is frittered away by detail. . . . Simplify, simplify." Even in the late nineteenth century, people were feeling the need to uncomplicate their lives! If Thoreau could see us now, he probably would have stayed in Walden. Then again, after seeing a recent news photograph of the crowded beach on Walden Pond, maybe not!

When I hear the word *simplify*, my mind invariably drifts to external simplification: cleaning out closets and drawers, reducing the clutter in my home and eliminating unnecessary activities that consume my time. And while all of these exercises are worthwhile, they only address the symptoms of the real problem.

I have been known, from time to time, to get vocal about how much time I seem to spend taking care of "stuff" rather than people. When I get like that, I usually start cleaning out and eliminating all kinds of clutter, only to discover that the problem is me, not the stuff! (Of course, my husband, Chuck, gets a little nervous when I get that way—he thinks I am going to make us all go live in the woods without telephones and electricity!) The truth is, if I am a slave to my "stuff" it is my own fault, and I want to be free from bondage in every way possible.

By now, we should have a clear understanding of what the word *simplify* means. In a complex world full of uncertainty and confusion, the concept sounds refreshing! The question is whether or not we are willing—or even able—to achieve simplicity in the twenty-first century. When we examine the intricate web of relationships, responsibilities and requirements inherent in modern culture, it might be easier to maintain the status quo rather than to simplify!

So how do we go about simplifying our lives? As much as I might enjoy living in a cabin in the woods, there is no getting away from God's mandate that we are to be in the world but not of it. Like it or not, I cannot be salt and light if I am not out there in the world, but that does not mean I have to contribute to the complications and chaos. Let me share an example of simplifying from my own experience.

A New Kind of Fast

It was the spring of 1979 when my husband, Chuck, and I stopped watching television and going to movies. We did not plan it, really; it just evolved through a series of circumstances. Like the Pevensie children in *The Lion, the Witch and the Wardrobe*, we were maneuvered by that unseen Hand into God's chosen fast for us.

We had gone to the movies with some friends to see a critically acclaimed film, *The Deer Hunter*, one Saturday afternoon. The theater was full of people, and we had to sit in one of the front rows. By the time the movie was over, I felt as if I had been imprisoned in a bamboo cage myself. As I walked out of the darkened building and into the late afternoon sunshine, waves of despair and depression had already overtaken me. I did not know it at the time, but I would not return to a theater until 1991, when our family went to see Disney's *The Rocketeer*.

My response to *The Deer Hunter* was actually the result of a reawakened conscience. For several years, I had indulged my darker sensibilities and turned a deaf ear to the promptings of the Holy Spirit when it came to entertainment. I read what I wanted and watched what I wanted, regardless of the

Voice inside that said to think on other things. I felt safe in my indulgences because I was a "born again" evangelical Christian who went to church once in a while.

In 1978, however, my life took a turn back toward things of the Spirit. My husband and I moved into a house in northwest Houston and found a new church. At that time, the congregation was in the process of finding a pastor. While the absence of a leader could have created an uncertain atmosphere, we found this place warm and welcoming. We met a group of people, all of them active in the life of that local body, who loved the Lord with all their hearts and were intimately acquainted with the Holy Spirit. Within months, their contagious faith and commitment had drawn us in and given us new purpose and direction.

Not long after *The Deer Hunter* experience, we noticed that we were not watching television anymore because we just did not have time for it. We were consumed with personal and corporate Bible study, and with prayer and fellowship with a new circle of friends. By the end of the summer in 1979, we had unplugged the television and given it away. I never regretted it. The reality of Philippians 4:8 had begun to work its way into our home, and television was the first casualty:

> Finally, brethren, whatever things are true, whatever things are noble, whatever things are just, whatever things are pure, whatever things are lovely, whatever things are of good report, if there is any virtue and if there is anything praiseworthy— meditate on these things.

Eventually we realized that we were in the midst of God's chosen fast for us. We were familiar with the practice of fasting from food and understood its validity for the believer, but this was something new. God had orchestrated events in our lives that culminated in a fast from secular entertainment. In Isaiah 58:6, God told the prophet that He would choose the fast for His people. The kind of fast God ordained would be "to loose the bonds of wickedness, to undo the heavy burdens, to let the oppressed go free."

Ultimately, God's chosen fast will produce light and healing in the believer's life. For the next several years, we did not watch television, go to movies, listen to secular music or even read secular books. During that time, we experienced a whole new world without the noise from the outside. We also saw the hand of God move in our lives in some amazing ways:

- We were both baptized in the Holy Spirit.
- The Word of God came to life.
- God opened our eyes to the reality of spiritual warfare.
- We experienced supernatural healing: Chuck from a mysterious growth on his optic nerve, and me from barrenness.
- We recognized the validity of God's promises for our personal lives.

Would we have seen and experienced these things if we had not been fasting from secular entertainment? I am convinced that we would not have. During that season, God chose to simplify our lives in ways that we never would have chosen or imagined. If God had put His finger on secular entertainment and said, "Give this up," I probably would have reasoned it away and found a loophole! I enjoyed my movies, my television shows, my popular music and my murder mysteries. Instead, God first embedded His Word and His people into our lives so that we transitioned into the fast gradually. By the time we realized what was happening, we had found something we enjoyed abundantly more than secular entertainment!

Breaking the Fast

As I said earlier, we did not step back into a movie theater until 1991. We did bring the television back sooner, but even that was a challenge! It was 1985. In the intervening years, we had adopted our first child, Daniel, as an infant. God had also healed me of barrenness, and we had a baby girl named Rebekah. When Chuck and I left the children's home in 1984, one of the teen boys from our cottage left with us. Although we were never able to legally adopt Joseph—his father was not willing to give him up completely—he is our son in every sense of the word. By March 1986, we would bring our fourth child, John Mark, home from the hospital. Even though we had enjoyed our fast from television, we knew that it was time for the fast to end. So Chuck bought a television.

We plugged the television in, turned it on and adjusted the antenna. We got five channels: ABC, CBS, NBC, PBS and a local UHF channel. Before long, it was obvious that we would be watching PBS more than any other channel. Daniel watched every nature show that came on, as well as *Sesame Street* and *Mister Rogers*. It would not be long before Rebekah and John Mark joined him.

By this time, the VCR had become so popular with the American consumer that we thought, *Why not?* The idea of taping programs so that we could watch them when we actually had the time—and the inclination—appealed to us. Chuck purchased our first VCR and several blank tapes. We hooked it up and set it to record a nature program on PBS that Wednesday night while we were at church.

On Thursday morning, we anxiously turned on the television, rewound the tape in the VCR and pressed "play." As the image appeared on the screen and the music began to play, Chuck completely freaked out.

"What's wrong?" I asked.

"I can't take it," he responded.

"Can't take what?" I asked, baffled.

"Doesn't it bother you? It's like Big Brother right here in our house!"

"Big Brother?" I asked. "You mean George Orwell's Big Brother?"

"Exactly," he exclaimed. "They can use the airwaves, turn on the TV when we aren't home and know exactly what we're doing."

Obviously, Chuck was not ready to take the plunge into the world of time-shift television viewing. The mysterious "They" were invading our home through the television, and it was more than he could accept. In many ways, it was like breaking a water-only fast with a steak and loaded baked potato when a wiser choice would be chicken noodle soup! We would have to transition back into the world one step at a time, so that was the end of our first VCR. It would be over a year before we tried it again.

Over twenty years have passed since we brought the television back into the house. When Chuck was ready to try a VCR again, movie rental businesses had popped up on every corner. Gradually, we reacquainted ourselves with the lost decade of Disney movies. Chuck was even able to overcome his paranoia and record programs without fear of Big Brother. The novelty of in-home movie viewing entertained and intrigued us and our children, and we discovered new ways to use recorded media for education and enrichment.

Our fast from secular entertainment served our family in many ways. Because we had fasted from secular entertainment for so long, we were more sensitive to undesirable elements in the videos we brought into the house. I will be forever grateful that the Lord did this work in us during the time when our children were young and impressionable. Beyond the obvious benefit of renewing our consciences, it also simplified our lives and freed up large blocks of time that had previously been wasted.

I have wondered many times if movies and television are a suitable form of entertainment for Christians. Obviously, we need to exercise discernment any time we indulge in entertainment. I am reminded, however, of one very important fact: Jesus recognized the value of entertainment when He taught His disciples. The parables are full of vivid imagery, colorful characters and insightful incidents that help believers understand Kingdom concepts and principles. Jesus Himself knew that our God-given imaginations would thrive on a great story told with purpose!

Faith, Focus and Function

When God maneuvered us into our fast from secular entertainment in 1979, we responded to Him by faith and followed His lead. We did not sit down, take a hard look at our leisure habits and recognize our need for a fast. Instead, God used circumstances to rearrange our time and our choices so that He could infuse new life into our desensitized consciences. Once Chuck and I recognized what was happening, we chose to enter into the God-ordained fast by faith. That response of faith led to focus and function. We learned to look at entertainment through a holy lens. Because of this faith-based focus, we enjoyed a season of simplified function in our lives.

It is amazing how much more time one has to manage when unnecessary entertainment is eliminated!

✴ We cannot always expect God to initiate fasts that lead to the discipline of simplification. By definition, a *discipline* is "training expected to produce a specific character or pattern of behavior, especially training that produces moral or mental improvement."[1] In other words, the spiritual discipline of simplicity is intended to improve our character and behavior both spiritually and mentally. Simplicity is not just an exercise in organization—it is a vital part of the Spirit-filled life. As sincere believers, we are responsible to activate our minds, wills and emotions and pursue God with all our hearts. That kind of pursuit includes thoughtful, deliberate cooperation with the Holy Spirit regarding our transformation.

When we get honest with ourselves about simplification, we can put faith into action. One thing all of us can do is inventory our lives. Do not panic! I am not advocating a legalistic accounting of activities down to the hour and minute. Instead, we want to make our lives available to the Holy Spirit so that He can highlight areas of concern. Everyone has the same number of days, hours and minutes in a week. God, on the other hand, has all the time in the world, so it makes sense to keep Him in the loop during this exercise.

Since we have been focusing on fasting from entertainment, let's start by considering some current statistics on American media habits. According to data collected by ACNielsen company, the average American watches over four hours of television every day—28 hours a week. But that is just the tip of the iceberg when it comes to our electronic media addiction. The following information was posted on the Digital Home website:

> The average American watches more than 151 hours of TV
> per month, an all-time high, according to a new report from

The Nielsen Company. In addition, the research firms found that Americans who watch video over the Internet consume another 3 hours of online video per month and those who use mobile video watch nearly 4 hours per month on mobile phones and other devices. In addition, Nielsen reported that the time spent watching recorded shows on a personal video recorder and other timeshifted television is watched at double the pace as video online at 7 hours, 11 minutes per month. Yet in a potential indicator of how audiences could timeshift in the future, young adults (age 18–24) watch video on the Internet and on a DVR at the same rate—about 5 hours per month. "The American fascination with television and other video content is not easing up, as consumers keep turning to TV, Internet and Mobile at record levels," said Susan Whiting, vice chair of The Nielsen Company.[2]

How much time do we spend on electronic media within a seven-day period? We will probably be surprised once we take a serious look at our habits. Keep in mind that we want to evaluate all of our electronic consumption, not just television. That means we must evaluate how much time we spend on the Internet (other than for work) and how much time we spend watching DVDs or recorded television shows (even educational programming).

Now What?

Evaluating the time we spend on electronic media is a lot like keeping a food diary. It is a bit of a shock writing down every bite one takes in a 24-hour period. The same is true when we keep track of how many hours we spend every day connected to the world via digital images! Even so, we owe it to ourselves and to our Father to get real about how we spend the time He has given us.

You may decide, after this accounting exercise, to take the next step and try a media fast. If you do, let me suggest a few options:

1. If you are really feeling motivated, try eliminating everything for a week. Of course, when I say everything, I do not mean you cannot check your email or use the Internet for work and essential research. But is television really necessary? Just try life without it. You might like it.

2. If you are not ready to tackle a full week, just try one day without electronic media of any kind. Again, it is okay if you have to access your email or the Internet for work.

3. Choose one form of electronic media at a time and eliminate it for a day, two days or even a week. This option is a little less painful than the first two!

4. Once you choose an option, use the time normally spent on electronic media doing something completely different. For example, if you normally spend two hours watching television in the evening, use that two hours to take a walk with a friend, prayer-walk your neighborhood or pick up a long-abandoned hobby.

5. Keep track of the time you reclaim from electronic media during your fast. I am always amazed at my options when I choose not to watch TV for an hour. Sometimes it is refreshing just to bask in the quiet for a little while!

6. Even if you return to your old habits, choose one day a week to fast from one or all types of electronic media. Many people do the same thing with a food fast for their intestinal health. It could not hurt to give our overloaded senses a rest from all that information once a week!

The point of this exercise is to allow the Holy Spirit access to our everyday lives. Electronic media is only one area that we might want to evaluate. Each person's lifestyle, work habits and interests present different challenges when it comes to simplification. While one person might squander hours a day watching television, another person might ignore his family and friends because he brings his work home every night. Neither extreme is balanced, nor do they exemplify a life of simplicity. We can achieve balance when we walk by faith, focus on God's best and operate in the function of simplicity. The question is, are we willing to submit to the Father and find that place of balance?

Do you remember the big Hollywood writers' strike of 2007–2008? While the writers were on strike, we were forced into another unplanned fast from television. As a result, our lives were simplified by the absence of something that could potentially clutter our lives. We discovered, once again, that secular entertainment was something we could live without. We spent more time together playing games, walking the dogs and reading books, simply because the easier choice of television was unavailable!

What clutters your life? Is it secular—or even Christian—entertainment, overuse of the Internet, too many commitments, too much stuff? When we honestly evaluate how we spend our leisure time, we discover potential time for those activities and people that truly matter. The Father can and will "teach us to number our days, that we may gain a heart of wisdom" (Psalm 90:12), if we are willing to open our eyes and ears to truth—truth about ourselves and the chaotic world in which we live.

4

Simplicity and the Law of Love

As we will learn in Chuck's chapters on anxiety, some of the same factors that trigger anxiety also directly affect our ability to live simply in the world. Several factors can contribute to a state of unrest and unbelief, and those same factors can complicate our lives. One of the most obvious— and most important—factors involved in both simplification and anxiety (or the lack of it) is how we relate to people.

Whenever I hear the word *people*, I am instantly reminded of a line from the movie *Singin' in the Rain*. I do not want to assume that everyone has seen this national treasure, so I will briefly summarize: At the height of the silent movie era, two actors—Lina Lamont and Don Lockwood—are enjoying tremendous success. Suddenly, the movie studio for which they work is thrown into a panic because another studio releases *The Jazz Singer*, a new movie set apart from all others because it is a "talkie." Every studio in Hollywood then prepares to enter the world of talking movies. Don Lockwood and his friend suggest that their studio turn their current production into a musical.

The only problem is that Lina's voice is high-pitched and annoying when she talks, and her singing is even worse. She is better off in silent movies! So Don and his friend devise an ingenious plan—they will dub over Lina's voice with the lovely voice of Don's girlfriend, Kathy. When Lina realizes what is going on, she is furious. Soon it is clear that Kathy deserves a career of her own, but Lina refuses to share the limelight. She threatens to sue, insisting that Kathy stay in the background to overdub parts. The studio head refuses to comply, saying that such a move would mean no career for Kathy. "Lina," he protests, "people just don't do that!"

"People!" Lina shouts in her irritating squeak. "I ain't *people!*" Then Lina reads from a newspaper article that she provided as publicity: "I am a 'shimmering, glowing star in the cinema firmament.' It says so—right here!"

Unlike characters in a movie, we cannot toss people aside just because they complicate our lives or get in the way of our grand schemes! On the contrary, the beautiful variety of people in our lives provides the framework for experiencing the love and grace of the Father. Granted, people sometimes provide some interesting challenges in life, but challenge is what presses us into the mercy and provision of the Savior!

People Are Complicated!

People are anything but simple. From a young age, we collect emotional, mental and spiritual baggage that weighs us down and hinders our fellowship with other people. That same baggage creates barriers between us and our loving Father. Simplicity, in its truest form, whittles away at that baggage so we can be restored to proper communion with the Lord.

In *Singin' in the Rain*, Lina Lamont had her own rules of conduct. After years of silent film success, she had begun to believe her own publicity. She was, after all, a "shimmering, glowing star in the cinema firmament." When a lowly chorus girl got in the way of her future success, Lina did not have to operate in the law of love or even the law of common courtesy! Somewhere along the way, Lina had collected baggage that dictated the way she related to people, and she felt she was not subject to the same rules as "people."

Not long before Jesus faced death on the cross, He gave His disciples a new law in John 13:34–35: "A new commandment I give to you, that you love one another; as I have loved you, that you also love one another. By this all will know that you are My disciples, if you have love for one another." When Jesus spoke these words, His disciples had no idea just how much Jesus loved them—yet. But Jesus knew exactly what this new commandment would require: His death. For Jesus, love would lead to the ultimate sacrifice on the cross. For His disciples, it would mean death to self.

Loving the way Jesus loves includes choosing to submit our flesh to the Word and will of the Father as we relate to other people. We all know how complicated, challenging and wonderful people can be. Living with other people, whether in a family, a church or the workplace, presents us with opportunities to demonstrate the love of Jesus in every situation. Because living with people can be complicated by so many factors, it is vital that we learn to apply the principles of simplification to our relationships.

Before I share a beautiful testimony about simplicity and the law of love in action, let's review the definitions of *simplify* once again:

- To make simple or simpler
- To reduce to basic essentials

- To diminish in scope or complexity—streamline
- To make more intelligible—clarify

Quite often, circumstances make it essential to simplify for the sake of those we love. The testimony that follows illustrates how one family streamlined their lives in a time of crisis in order to minister to and care for someone they loved.

Compelled by Love

In an earlier chapter, I referred to the church Chuck and I attended in the late 1970s and 1980s. During the nine years we were part of that fellowship in northwest Houston, we were blessed with some deep and lasting relationships with other believers. One family we grew to love and cherish was the Kellers: James, Jan and their three children. James and Jan were—and still are—passionate in their faith and full of life, but Jan has the added distinction of being the most compassionate and loving person I have ever met.

Initially, Chuck had his doubts about whether or not it was possible for someone to be as precious as Jan seemed to be. It was not long before even my cynical husband was convinced that Jan was the genuine article. Over the years, both the Kellers and the Pierces left Houston and moved to opposite regions of Texas: the Kellers to McAllen in south Texas, and the Pierces to Denton in North Texas. In spite of our distance from each other, we maintained our friendship and have managed to stay connected through the years. We keep informed about the three Keller children (now grown, married and raising their own families), and Jan and James are always interested in (and praying for) our two teenagers, four married children and their families.

In February 2008, the Kellers' son, John, was involved in a devastating motorcycle accident in McAllen, Texas. Within hours, the call to pray had gone out all over the state and beyond. By February 24, the Keller family had already started an online blog[1] to keep everyone apprised of John's condition and progress. Here's the first entry in the blog:

John Keller was in a motorcycle accident on February 17th at 1:30 pm. He was hit by a car pulling out of a shopping center on 10th Street in north McAllen. He was rushed to McAllen Medical Center because he had sustained serious head injury and a broken pelvis. To catch you up to date on what has happened in the past week:

2-17-08—John had both brain surgery to remove a blood clot, and pelvic surgery to fix 3 fractures in his pelvis. They put him in an induced coma to reduce the swelling to his brain.

2-18-08—John is resting this day. We are watching 24 hours a day.

2-19-08—John is still resting and we are praying. Prayer, worship, and ministry in the waiting room.

2-20-08—John goes for his second surgery. More prayer, worship, and more ministry.

2-21-08—John is resting and looking better.

2-22-08—John goes for his third surgery. Jesus said the bleeding has stopped.

2-23-08—Great day for John. He is stable and he is showing movement when they reduced the dosage of the sedative.

2-24-08—John is looking great. More color and is stable. There is also talk of moving him to Houston's Methodist Hospital.

The first thing I noticed as I began to read the blog was the overwhelming tone of faith in each entry. Of course, knowing the Keller family, I was not surprised by this fact. One entry on the blog referred to a word that Jan had received regarding her son:

> We began this walk standing on His word. John's mom, Jan, had been given a word from 2 Kings 4:26. She was like the Shunammite woman whose son hurt his head. The man of God saw her and said to her, "Is it well with you? Is it well with your husband? Is it well with the child?" And she answered, "It is well."

By February 26, John was transferred to Methodist Hospital in Houston. In the months that followed, John's family and friends adjusted their schedules, eliminated unnecessary activity and *simplified* their lives in order to be available as needed. John's young family, along with his parents, in-laws, siblings, extended family and friends, rallied by faith and focused on that day when John would be restored.

The kind of simplification required in times like this is not easy. Indeed, simplifying one's daily routine in the midst of devastating circumstances is anything but easy. In situations like John Keller's, simplification means temporary housing in another city, depending on help with small children, learning to participate in recovery. Simplification is not always about making life easier; instead, it is often much more difficult than the normal. Because of this family's love for John, they were all willing to reduce their routines to basic essentials, diminish other responsibilities in scope and complexity, and streamline in order to focus on whatever God required.

What equips us to face trouble and simplify our lives for the sake of someone else? It is that new commandment: the law of love. Love enabled the Keller family to focus, by faith, on John's recovery. Love sustained this family from the hospital to the rehabilitation facility and beyond. Love enabled each friend and relative involved in John's journey

to simplify their lives enough to be available to pray, to visit
and to rejoice.

In May 2008, John opened his eyes. Then in January 2009,
the following report was posted on the blog:

> John is back home! He left TIRR [The Institute for Rehabilita-
> tion and Research] on Thursday morning and had a great trip
> in the front seat of the car! On the way down they stopped at
> Dairy Queen and John walked in and had a hamburger and
> fries. He said it feels so good to be normal again. . . . He is
> talking more and more and remembers everyone. People have
> been coming to visit and are blown away by how much he is
> saying and how much he remembers. He is walking a lot and
> has enjoyed watching the kids play and has sat outside quite a
> bit. He even went for a few rides in the golf cart today while
> holding Dalton, his youngest son. . . . John also has not used
> his wheelchair since he has been home. He just walks with
> someone by his side to assist him. It is amazing to see how
> far he has come and what a miracle he is.

On the anniversary of John's motorcycle accident, the
following update was posted:

> A year ago today John was hit on his motorcycle.
> "Tomorrow about this time things are going to change."
> Those words, which were spoken at the "Starting the Year
> off Right Conference" in Jan. 2008 with Chuck Pierce and
> Glory of Zion, have certainly marked our year. Pastor Joseph
> Garlington spoke those words as he taught us about decreeing
> and declaring over our lives when something happens that
> you are not ready for. His text was 2 Kings 4:8–26. This has
> been our walk and we are so blessed to see so many who have
> joined with us to pray for John and our entire family. It has
> been a miracle from day one and the miracle continues. "In a
> year, about this time, things are going to change." On January
> 29, 2009, we were dismissed from TIRR in Houston. John

began speaking on Wednesday the 21st the week earlier. He began eating on his own on that Sunday the 25th. He began walking on his own those weeks, also. John had agreed that he would walk out of that hospital as a testimony to God and he did. We rented a wheelchair, and to this day we have not used the chair—glory to God. They actually came and picked up the wheelchair today; isn't that prophetic! Jan had prayed that the wonderful folks at TIRR would get to see the miracle before we were checked out. They got to see John walk, talk, eat, and understand and call them by their names even though he had never spoken to them. They were all so amazed and blessed. We all know that it is because so many continued to pray and never give up. . . . Our God is not the "Great I Was" or the "Great I Used to Be," but He is still the GREAT I AM!

What a testimony to the love and mercy of our God! John's family and friends loved him enough to respond by faith, focus on the goal and restructure the function of their lives in order to cooperate with God in John's restoration.

Simplifying in the midst of devastation requires extraordinary submission to the Father and faith that, regardless of the outcome, He is good. Simplifying in the midst of ordinary, everyday living requires the same submission without the accompanying sense of urgency. Nevertheless, simplifying for the sake of love can present its own challenges.

Simply Loving, Day by Day

In chapter 1, we discussed Martha, Mary and choosing the "good part." Choosing the good part starts with evaluating priorities. Obviously, people are more important than things. Unfortunately, things—houses, jobs, hobbies, chores—often force themselves into the forefront and rob us of valuable time and energy that rightfully belong to friends, family, co-workers, the Lord and even ourselves. Please do not misunderstand me. I know that we have responsibilities, many of which benefit our friends and family, but we must examine our lives to determine whether or not we are submitting our time and efforts to the Holy Spirit. (Remember: God has all the time in the world, so He is an excellent resource when it comes to evaluating our time-management skills!)

For starters, here is a list to help us start evaluating our time and energy:

- List your top priorities. What is most important to you? What (or whom) do you value most?
- List your commitments. Consider everything, including work, church, household, family, children's extracurricular activities, hobbies, freelance work, even leisure time. Which of these commitments do you value most? Which of these fit into the top priorities you have already listed?
- Account for your time. How do you spend your waking hours? From the time you get up until the time you go to sleep, what are you doing with your time? Are you using any of your time for your top priorities?

This kind of evaluation can be difficult. Whether you are a CEO, a parent, a teacher, a construction worker or a minister, being honest about how you use your time every day is challenging. We all know that we should expend more time and energy on the people in our lives, but it is just so easy to get sidetracked by what we have come to consider urgent.

When my children were small, I waged a constant battle between what had to be done and what would really matter five, ten, even twenty years down the road. If you are (or have been) a parent, you know that children come with a whole new batch of household chores. They have to eat (surprise!), they get dirty, they get sick, they have homework and special class projects and they have to play. If you have more than one child, all of that is multiplied! But guess what? When our children are grown, it will not be our efficiency as housekeepers they will remember. Instead, it will be the little adventures along the way that required us to put aside the broom or the dishcloth in favor of a teepee in the backyard.

When I had five children under the age of ten, an experienced mother gave me one of the best pieces of advice I have ever received: She told me, "Go to the Laundromat!" Really! I will never forget the time when all the kids caught the same gastrointestinal virus within five days of each other. By the time it had run its course, my two-load pile of laundry had quickly evolved into an overwhelming ten-load mountain in the middle of the kitchen floor. I could have forced myself to tackle the mountain one load at a time, ignoring my recuperating children, but I chose to take my friend's advice instead. I loaded the kids and the laundry into the van. As soon as I had those ten loads swishing safely in commercial-sized washing machines, we went to the park. The fresh air and sunshine were good for all of us!

Now, go back to your list of priorities, commitments and time. Look closely at each thing on the list and consider this:

- Does this add meaning/value to my life?
- How important is this to me?
- Does this conflict with or enhance my priorities?
- Could I eliminate this from my life?

Once we honestly answer these questions, we need to take action. Just as I suggested in the chapter on fasting, choose one thing from your list that conflicts with your identified priorities and eliminate it. Start by eliminating that one thing for just a few days or a week, then reevaluate. It will not take long to determine if that one thing can be permanently removed from your list, thereby carving out a little more time for the people in your life.

It is important to keep in mind the motivation for evaluating our time commitments and priorities—love. When we approach this evaluation with the three keys of simplification—faith, focus and function—we can be confident that the Holy Spirit will be controlling the pencil.

The Father's love compels us to choose the good part so that we do not miss the precious treasures He has placed within each of His children. Before we move on to the next chapter, let's examine some common obstacles that get in the way of connecting with the people in our lives.

Multitasking, Technology and Stress

I have a few confessions to make before starting this section: I do not multitask unless it is absolutely necessary, I am not a huge fan of technology and I try to avoid situations that create stress in my life. Now then, let's look at multitasking, technology and stress and their impact on our relationships!

The computer age has thrown us all into a new way of functioning. Years ago, when someone used the word *multitasking*, it was a reference to the simultaneous operation by a computer's CPU of two or more tasks. Now we use that word to refer to a human being doing the same thing as a computer! Of course, we all juggle more than one thing at a time to some degree. (Watch any mother of small children if you want an example of multitasking that has nothing to do with computers!) The question is, how does habitual multitasking affect us and the people we love?

A recent headline on America Online had this to say about multitasking:

> We all multitask, a necessary survival skill of the digital age. But did you know that just listening to the news while you answer your e-mail can limit how well you're able to recall both? Normally, when you take in new information, you process it with a part of the brain called the cerebral cortex. "But multitasking greatly reduces learning because people can't attend to the relevant information," says UCLA psychology professor and memory researcher Russell Poldrack, Ph.D. That's because the brain is forced to switch processing to an area called the striatum, and the information stored here tends to contain fewer important details. Luckily, this kind of memory problem has an easy fix, says Poldrack: Simply pay undivided attention to whatever you really want to recall later.[2]

Multitasking and spending quality time with friends and family do not mix. We might think we can listen to the details of our daughter's first day in high school while checking our phone messages and making a grocery list, but the truth is that one of those things will get lost in the shuffle. We will either misunderstand our daughter, delete an important message or forget the milk. Hopefully, it will not be the first one!

When all of my children were still living at home, on many days we seemed to live in the minivan. At that time, none of the kids had a cell phone or an iPod. As long as we were driving, they were my prisoners. I had discovered, when Daniel was a teenager, that my children would open up and say almost anything to the back of my head that they would never say to my face. Because of this interesting phenomenon, I drove all over town without turning on the radio so that I could really hear my children. To this day, some of the most honest and enlightening conversations I ever had with my children took place in the car while I was driving to baseball, piano lessons or church. Had I been preoccupied with the car radio or a cell phone, I would have missed so much!

With the inundation of cell phones and iPods comes competition for time and attention in the car. Of course, my children are all driving themselves these days, but I still do not use my cell phone while driving. I am one of those strange people for whom driving demands my full attention. Besides, now I have grandchildren in the backseat, and that precious cargo deserves my best attention—driving and otherwise! Who knows, one of these days, my grandchildren might be telling their deepest secrets to the back of my head.

Modern multitasking is directly related to the mushroom cloud of technology available today. There are just so many fun toys to play with these days! Even though I am not a huge fan of technology, I can certainly appreciate and understand the fascination. All of my children have cell phones, some of them have iPhones, and most of them use iPods rather than CDs. My two youngest sons have developed calluses from text messaging. I do not even know how to send a text message!

Technology, in and of itself, is neither good nor evil. It is just technology. My only real issue with technology comes when it interferes with what is truly valuable: time with family, friends and our heavenly Father. If some modern innovation simplifies our lives and actually results in more time for what matters, I am all for it. My concern is that, like R. Buckminster Fuller said, "Humanity is acquiring all the right technology for all the wrong reasons."

Simplifying our lives does not have to mean ditching technology in favor of two cups at the ends of a string. It does mean we need to establish some boundaries when it comes to the use of all those wonderful gadgets. Let's consider doing the following:

- Turn off the cell phone when we do not want (or should not want!) to be contacted. That includes when we are enjoying time with our family or friends.

- Leave the cell phone behind when we want to focus on a loved one or friend. For example, when a friend or family member needs some quality time with us to share personal thoughts or problems, let's be mindful of how precious that time is. (Remember Lina Lamont and the laws of common courtesy!)

- A family vacation needs to be just that. Leave the work behind and focus on the people we love.

- Consider screening calls by using caller ID, or just let the answering machine take calls when necessary.

- For those of us who watch television, use a DVR to record and play back programs. (I am continually grateful for that little gadget! Chuck and I can watch a thirty-minute episode of *Jeopardy* in less than twenty minutes. That is a quick brain workout!)

One good reason to reduce our multitasking and preoccupation with technology is the fact that both of these contribute to stress. The dictionary defines *stress* as "a mentally or emotionally disruptive or upsetting condition occurring in response to adverse external influences and usually characterized by increased heart rate, a rise in blood pressure, muscular tension, irritability, and depression."[3] (See why I try to avoid situations that create stress in my life?) Of course, a myriad of situations and triggers cause stress. If we can reduce stress even a little bit by limiting multitasking and invasive technology, we should give it a try!

One stressor associated with technology is caused by information overload. Twenty-four-hour news, the Internet, cell phones with streaming video—personally, I neither want nor need that much information! We need to guard our hearts and minds from those things that rob our joy and create unnecessary anxiety. Let's take seriously the words of Proverbs 4:23: "Above all else, guard your heart, for it is the wellspring of life" (NIV).

It is time for all of us to evaluate how our busy lives affect the people God has put in our lives. Let's simplify by faith, focus on what truly matters to the Father and move into a new realm of Spirit-led function. We will all be better for choosing the good part!

5

Simplicity, Sabbath and Refreshing

Every day, we make choices about how we will live our lives. Sometimes the choices are obvious and uncomplicated, like whether or not to show up for work. After all, the apostle Paul told the Thessalonians, "If anyone will not work, neither shall he eat" (2 Thessalonians 3:10). Other choices, however, require a more considered approach. We are free to choose life over death, obedience over rebellion, simplicity over complication. When we face choices, it is wise to consider the words of Micah 6:8: "He has shown you, O man, what is good; and what does the LORD require of you but to do justly, to love mercy, and to walk humbly with your God?"

Humility is a central characteristic of simplicity. Humility is the opposite of pride, which separates us from God and our fellow man. Choosing to walk humbly with our God involves submitting to His direction and turning a deaf ear to our own prideful course. When we insist on following our own prideful course, we lose the simplicity that is in Christ.

Walking humbly with our God, however, provides us with opportunities to experience simplicity in the midst of our busy, often chaotic lives.

The Sabbath Rest

Over the centuries, God has given His people countless opportunities to enter into blessing through obedience. One example of this is God's institution of the Sabbath rest. In 2006, my pastor, Dr. Robert Heidler, wrote a book entitled *The Messianic Church Arising! Restoring the Church to Our Covenant Roots*. Before the book was published, Robert asked me to proofread the manuscript one last time. With red pencil in hand, I sat down one morning and dove into the book, prepared to put my technical writing experience to work. Instead, I experienced a mini revival as I learned what the Church has lost over the last two thousand years. For centuries now, much of the rich heritage God intended to pass to His Body through the Hebrew people has been ignored or discarded for one reason or another.

In Robert's book, one chapter called "Entering God's Rest: The Principle of the Sabbath" explains the cycle of the Sabbath blessing. The observance of Sabbath—or *Shabbat*—was one of God's first directives for His new creation in the Garden of Eden. From the beginning, God intended people, animals and the land itself to enjoy the benefits of a Sabbath rest. In Genesis 2:2–3 we read, "By the seventh day God had finished the work he had been doing; so on the seventh day he rested from all his work. And God blessed the seventh day and made it holy, because on it he rested from all the work of creating that he had done" (NIV).

In spite of this clear directive, however, many of God's people choose not to follow the biblical pattern for rest instituted in the Garden. Our busy lives conspire against Sabbath. The idea of losing a day for the sake of resting seems almost criminal to some of us. We have so much to do and only so many waking hours during which to accomplish it. In spite of all the modern appliances and innovations designed to ease our daily tasks, we seem to have less and less time available to enjoy life. As my pastor notes in his book, "Our laborsaving devices cannot produce a life of rest because work always expands to fill time available. The key to rest is not found in laborsaving devices. The key to rest is found in the Word of God. True rest begins with God's gift of Sabbath."[1]

The good news is that we do not have to continue running down the same path. We can choose to embrace the blessing of Sabbath by consciously simplifying a few elements in our lives. But first, let's increase our understanding of the Sabbath. As my pastor explains in his chapter on Sabbath, the Creator took a day off after the six days of creation and rested. We know, of course, that the Master and Creator of the universe did not need to rest. Instead, He *chose* to rest in order to establish a pattern for His creation. As Dr. Heidler explains, God "wanted the principle of Sabbath woven into the fabric of the universe."[2]

The concept of Sabbath, then, is a good thing for mankind. Unfortunately for us, the pattern has been for man to ignore the blessing of Sabbath and work instead. We have allowed unbelief, fear and greed to interfere with the God-ordained order of work and rest. For that reason, God sought to protect the blessing of Sabbath with the law. My pastor explains that the way God chose to protect *Shabbat* is very significant: When God gave the "Law of the Sabbath," He did not give it as a *civil law* for the nation of Israel. Nor was it one of the *ceremonial laws* governing Jewish religious ritual. It was given as part of God's *moral law* for mankind. God made the observance of Sabbath one of the Ten Commandments. That means it is just as much a violation of God's moral law to work seven days a week as it is to kill, steal or commit adultery.[3]

A Mindset for Sabbath

When we consider the severity of ignoring the Sabbath, we must adjust our thinking about rest. Once we know God's truth about any issue, we are responsible to change our way of doing things. Just because I think I am too busy to observe the Sabbath according to God's plan for blessing does not mean I am justified in my sin. Let's be honest about this: Violating God's moral law is sin, and sin leads to a breakdown in communion and a loss of blessing.

I recently read a book called *Redeeming Creation: The Biblical Basis for Environmental Stewardship*. The four Christian biologists who authored it share another insight into Sabbath. They recognize that God did not rest out of need, but out of a desire to enjoy what He had just created. Like an artist, God chose to step back and admire His handiwork while continuing to sustain and nurture it. The authors proceed with this New Covenant perspective:

> The New Testament speaks of this rest as Jesus "seated" after his finished work of redemption in order to give to others the benefits of his work (Hebrews 8:1; 10:12). Likewise, the New Testament gives a call to all Christians to make this rest a part of their own lives, and enter into it through faith in Christ (Hebrews 4:1). To observe the Sabbath is for all the created order to recognize that it came from God and belongs to him forever, the recipient of his blessing. That is why God's laws concerning the Sabbath were never confined to people, but explicitly included animals and the land itself.[4]

As believers, we need to change our attitudes and actions regarding Sabbath to reflect this New Covenant perspective.

As a teenager in a traditional Christian home, I understood that Sundays—what we called the Sabbath— were reserved for church attendance, family dinner and quiet pastimes. I rarely asked to go to the lake or to a movie with friends on a Sunday afternoon, and chores (other than washing dishes by hand) were put off until Monday morning. Because Sundays were, quite honestly, a bore, I felt no great compulsion to continue this traditional observance beyond high school. It was not until I began to understand and observe the original, biblical pattern for Sabbath that I welcomed the blessing back into my life.

For me—and many other Christians—the Sabbaths of my childhood were not days of celebration and restoration. Instead, they were boring days to be endured and dreaded. The good news is that we do not have to follow that template when we receive God's blessing of Sabbath. Instead, the Sabbath God has ordained for His people is one we can look forward to with anticipation and joy. As my pastor says, "The true picture of Sabbath is a day of celebration, a day to turn the burdens of life over to God and enjoy His goodness. God intended Sabbath to be a blessing, not a burden. In Mark 2:27, Jesus said, 'The Sabbath was made for man, not man for the Sabbath.'"[5]

How, then, are we to simplify our lives enough to consistently observe the Sabbath and benefit from its blessing? The first step is, as always, one of faith: We must believe that God's plan for the Sabbath rest is for our benefit. The Sabbath is not meant to be another burden in our busy lives. On the contrary, when implemented from the perspective of faith, the Sabbath is a gracious gift from our loving Father. Here are two promises from the Word of God regarding the Sabbath:

If you keep your feet from breaking the Sabbath
and from doing as you please on my holy day,
if you call the Sabbath a delight
and the LORD's holy day honorable,
and if you honor it by not going your own way
and not doing as you please or speaking idle
words,

then you will find your joy in the LORD,
and I will cause you to ride on the heights of the
land
and to feast on the inheritance of your father
Jacob.

Isaiah 58:13–14, NIV

Foreigners who bind themselves to the LORD
to serve him,
to love the name of the LORD,
and to worship him,
all who keep the Sabbath without desecrating it
and who hold fast to my covenant—

these I will bring to my holy mountain
and give them joy in my house of prayer.

Isaiah 56:6–7, NIV

From Faith to Focus

Once we agree with God, by faith, concerning Sabbath, we can focus our hearts and minds on the next step: sifting through the twenty-first-century madness to find the time and the place for Sabbath. Let's return to *The Messianic Church Arising!* for my pastor's personal testimony about Sabbath:

Several years ago the Lord convicted me to begin observing a weekly Sabbath. He impressed me to follow the biblical pattern, observing Sabbath from sundown Friday till sundown Saturday.

When the Lord first convicted me of this, I resisted. I said, "Lord, I can't do that." As a pastor, Saturday was often my busiest day of the week. Weekdays at our church office are so filled with appointments and administrative duties that Saturday was often the only day I had to prepare for my Sunday message.

I said, "Lord, I'm too busy. I don't have time to take a day of rest." I thought, with horror, of having to stand up on Sunday morning with no message to give.

But the Lord answered, "To say you are too busy to rest on the Sabbath is like saying you are too poor to tithe. It means you have not yet learned My ability to provide. If I tell you to rest, you CAN rest."

So I chose to cast my concerns on Him and submit to His direction. I began to welcome Sabbath as a wonderful gift of God. There have been many times that Friday evening comes and my work is not done, and I have to place it, by faith, in His hands. But He has never failed to provide what I need.[6]

Functioning in Sabbath Rest

Once we are convinced that keeping the Sabbath is a good thing to do, we are ready to learn to function in biblical Sabbath. We move from faith, through focus, into function. At this point, we can ask ourselves, *How do I observe the Sabbath?* The answer to that question depends entirely on you and the unique conditions of your life. The primary requirement for observing the Sabbath is to rest from your regular work (see Leviticus 23:3). Other than that, we are all free to enter into the blessing of Sabbath as God leads each one of us!

My pastor makes the following observation about the Sabbath:

Sabbath is a day to avoid doing what you normally do to earn your living. It means you are freed from your normal responsibilities and given time to fellowship with God and enjoy His goodness!

I suspect that "proper Sabbath activity" varies from person to person. If you are a farmer, you wouldn't want to spend Sabbath working in your garden. But if you spend the rest of the week chained to a computer, a few hours of gardening on a Saturday morning might be a wonderful way to rest and enjoy the Lord.

Wayne Muller described Sabbath activity as "Time consecrated to enjoy and celebrate what is beautiful and good— time to light candles, sing songs, worship, tell stories, bless our children and loved ones, give thanks, share meals, nap, walk, and even make love. It is a time to be nourished and refreshed as we let our work, our chores and our important projects lie fallow, trusting that there are larger forces at work taking care of the world when we are at rest."[7]

I do not know about you, but a Sabbath rest is starting to sound good to me right now! In order to enter into this Sabbath rest, however, we have to prepare by simplifying our routine leading into the observance of Sabbath. In other words, if we choose to practice the biblical pattern for Sabbath, we will need to clear our calendar of regular activities and responsibilities and make plans with the people who will be sharing the Sabbath with us. For parents, that means including the children in planning. For singles, it might involve inviting some friends to participate in one way or another. In my church, several single people share at least a portion of the Sabbath with one another. What a beautiful way to fellowship!

Generally, one starts the Sabbath observance with the evening meal on a Friday night (or a night of your own choosing). For many families, this might be one of the few family dinners during the week. Initially, this may present a challenge for the overextended teenagers in the house. Just keep in mind that this is worth doing. Involve the children in the planning, share the benefits of Sabbath rest and let the Lord complete the work. As you begin to make room for *Shabbat* in your own life, consider the following elements:

- Clear the schedule—set this time apart from the rest of the week.
- Keep the meals simple—unless you really enjoy cooking and cleaning up afterward, choose foods that are easy to prepare, fun to eat and easy to clean up.
- Plan enjoyable activities.
- Invite friends or other family members to start the celebration on Friday night.
- Take time to express gratitude and praise to God with a heart of worship.
- Continue enjoying the blessing of *Shabbat* on Saturday with whatever brings you and your family/friends joy.

Remember that God ordained the Sabbath as a blessing. It is a time to rejoice in God, enjoy His creation and express thanksgiving for His goodness. It is not a legalistic, boring observance, but a celebration!

In the Pierce household, Friday night will usually include two or more extra bodies. That is never a problem for us— our sons know that their friends are welcome to join us in celebrating *Shabbat*. It is not intended to be an exclusive celebration that involves just the family while shutting others

81

out. Instead, it is a joyful occasion that can draw others into the benefits and blessing of Sabbath.

Creator, His Creation and Refreshing

It is no accident that the very first Sabbath rest occurred right after God completed His good work of creation. According to the biblical account,

> God saw everything that He had made, and indeed it was very good. So the evening and the morning were the sixth day.
> Thus the heavens and the earth, and all the host of them, were finished. And on the seventh day God ended His work which He had done, and He rested on the seventh day from all His work which He had done. Then God blessed the seventh day and sanctified it, because in it He rested from all His work which God had created and made.
>
> Genesis 1:31–2:3

It had been a busy, fruitful six days for the Creator of the universe. He started on day one by dividing the darkness from the light and moved right into separating the waters from the heavens on the second day. On the third day, things really got moving. Not only did God separate the seas from the dry land, but He demonstrated His artistic nature by filling the earth with every imaginable species of plant. On the fourth day, God set the heavens ablaze with the stars, the moon, the sun and distant planets in infinite galaxies. On the fifth day, God brought life forth from the waters, from great sea creatures to the tiniest hummingbird. By then, it was time for God to turn His attention to the land. From the earth He brought forth every other creature, ultimately shaping His masterpiece: man.

No wonder the Creator chose to rest on the seventh day. It was time to savor the beauty and diversity of all that He had created, including the first man and woman. Although the Genesis record does not include an account of how God, Adam and Eve spent that first Sabbath, I would imagine that it closely resembled the Creator's later instructions concerning the observance of *Shabbat*.

Can you imagine sitting down on a carpet of weed-free grass and sharing a meal of freshly picked fruits, vegetables, nuts and new wine with the Ancient of Days? Adam and Eve were brand-new, perfect humans, capable of unhindered communion with their Father. Not only had God given them life, but He had given them life in a perfectly beautiful environment. In spite of what was to come, that first Sabbath was a model for every Sabbath to come.

It is clear from Scripture that God's creation is precious to Him. Over and over in the first chapter of Genesis, the writer repeats, "And God saw that it was good." Psalm 104 provides a beautiful song of praise to the Creator for His creation:

> He sends the springs into the valleys;
> They flow among the hills.
> They give drink to every beast of the field;
> The wild donkeys quench their thirst.
> By them the birds of the heavens have their home;
> They sing among the branches.
> He waters the hills from His upper chambers;
> The earth is satisfied with the fruit of Your
> works. . . .
>
> O LORD, how manifold are Your works!
> In wisdom You have made them all.
> The earth is full of Your possessions—
> This great and wide sea,
> In which are innumerable teeming things,

Living things both small and great.
There the ships sail about;
There is that Leviathan
Which You have made to play there. . . .

May the glory of the LORD endure forever;
May the LORD rejoice in His works.

Psalm 104:10–13, 24–26, 31

If the Lord rejoices in His works, we should do the same. For that reason alone, we will benefit from including a little rejoicing in His creation as part of our Sabbath rest. But there are so many more reasons to experience the wonder and beauty of creation in the midst of *Shabbat*. Consider this example from one of the biologists who helped write the book I mentioned earlier, *Redeeming Creation*. He relates that when he was a college professor in Indiana, he would take small groups of students on trips into northern Michigan each fall. Rather than focusing on their class textbook, they would spend their time exploring living examples of the book's concepts—succession on sand dunes, the flow of groundwater into marshes, the formation of soil in a forest. In the evenings, they would study and reflect on God's Word as it related to the creation they were exploring.

Many students said the trips were the highlight of the course, which did not surprise their professor. What did surprise him was that many also described the trips as "the most powerful spiritual experience" they had during their entire time at college—a Christian college focused on preparation for ministry and Christian service, with chapel every day and entire days often set aside for special spiritual emphases. Yet those autumn excursions into the wonder of God's creation provided the students with their most moving and memorable displays of His power and glory.

As the professor commented, "It is wind and rain in the face on a treeless hill, the mud of a marsh beneath one's feet, and the sound of whirring wings at sunset that give examples of what joy and beauty *are*. . . . Joy must be a taste, a touch and a smell, not an idea only, and God must be not only the Lord of heaven above but also the Maker of earth beneath."[8]

Shabbat is an opportunity for us to "taste and see that the LORD is good" (Psalm 34:8). The goodness of God is apparent to anyone willing to get out of the house or the office and experience the beauty of God's handiwork up close and personal! But we must practice the art of simplicity in order to experience the fullness of the Sabbath rest. The complications and distractions of the world, our commitments and our tyrannical responsibilities war against our entering into God's blessing of *Shabbat*.

If you do not already observe Sabbath rest on a regular basis, I encourage you to give it a try. The blessing of Sabbath is just one more reward of simplicity. When we make the commitment to consciously simplify one day out of our busy week to rest according to God's definition, the benefits are tremendous.

I will close this chapter with one last word from my pastor, a man who really knows how to celebrate Sabbath:

> What happens if you miss a Sabbath? Some weekends I might be ministering at a conference and don't have the option of rest. What do I do if a week comes when I cannot celebrate the Sabbath?
>
> That's when I appreciate the grace of God. I remember that Sabbath is not a legalistic burden. When I miss Sabbath, I'm not filled with guilt. I'm filled with sorrow and disappointment. I have missed a blessing. . . .

85

But if you celebrate Sabbath as God intended, it will not be something you *have* to do—it is something you *want* to do. Real Sabbath observance is addictive.

God wants to make our walk with Him so enjoyable and so pleasurable that the world looks on with envy. . . . Receive God's GIFT of Sabbath.[9]

6

Money, Possessions and Simplicity

No examination of simplification would be complete without addressing the role of money and possessions in our lives and how they impact us. In the current atmosphere of economic uncertainty, our relationship to money becomes even more significant. Let's agree to be honest with the Lord and with ourselves as we examine the role of money and possessions in our lives, and let's take a closer look at how they affect our ability to simplify.

For the believer, any discussion about money has to begin with the Word of God. What does God say about money, possessions and the accumulation of wealth? According to the New Testament, God and money are two different masters. In Matthew 6:24, we read the following: "No one can serve two masters. Either he will hate the one and love the other, or he will be devoted to the one and despise the other. You cannot serve both God and Money" (NIV).

In the New King James Version of the Bible, the word *money* is translated "mammon" and sounds much more ominous! According to the dictionary, *mammon* is "riches, avarice, and worldly gain personified as a false god in the Bible."[1]

Jesus spent a lot of time talking about money when He walked the earth. Even though His disciples were not wealthy men, Jesus made certain that they were aware of the snares inherent in money and its pursuit. The following passage contains just one example of how Jesus communicated truth to His disciples:

> And He said to them, "Take heed and beware of covetousness, for one's life does not consist in the abundance of the things he possesses." Then He spoke a parable to them, saying: "The ground of a certain rich man yielded plentifully. And he thought within himself, saying, 'What shall I do, since I have no room to store my crops?' So he said, 'I will do this: I will pull down my barns and build greater, and there I will store all my crops and my goods. And I will say to my soul, "Soul, you have many goods laid up for many years; take your ease; eat, drink, and be merry."' But God said to him, 'Fool! This night your soul will be required of you; then whose will those things be which you have provided?'
>
> "So is he who lays up treasure for himself, and is not rich toward God."
>
> Then He said to His disciples, "Therefore I say to you, do not worry about your life, what you will eat; nor about the body, what you will put on. Life is more than food, and the body is more than clothing. Consider the ravens, for they neither sow nor reap, which have neither storehouse nor barn; and God feeds them. Of how much more value are you than the birds?"
>
> Luke 12:15–24

At first glance, the man in this parable does not appear guilty of any terrible crime that would warrant death. He had been blessed with fertile land and an abundance of produce, so he had to build a bigger barn! We know, however, that something was amiss because of God's response to his building program. Jesus compared the man in the parable to anyone "who lays up treasure for himself, and is not rich toward God." God called him a fool and required his life that very night! I think it would be safe to guess that the rich man was taking all the credit for his fertile ground and abundant crop. In his mind, God had nothing to do with his success. The rich man with the big barn had chosen his master, and it was not God.

In the gospel of Mark, Jesus tells the parable of the sower. The sower scattered the same good seed on different kinds of ground. "And some seed fell among thorns; and the thorns grew up and choked it, and it yielded no crop" (4:7). Later, after the crowds of people had left Jesus alone with His disciples, they asked Him what the parable meant. Jesus patiently explained that the seed represents the Word of God, and the different types of ground represent the different kinds of people who hear the Word. Jesus explained the significance of the seed sown among the thorns by saying, "Now these are the ones sown among thorns; they are the ones who hear the word, and the cares of this world, the deceitfulness of riches, and the desires for other things entering in choke the word, and it becomes unfruitful" (4:18–19).

The cares of this world, the *deceitfulness of riches* and *the desires for other things* choke the Word of God to the point of unfruitfulness. Deceitful riches and wanting things—things other than the Word of God—contribute to a life that produces no fruit. But how, exactly, can "riches" (money and possessions) be deceitful?

To deceive means to mislead or cause someone to believe what is not true. Riches, then, can mislead us and cause us

89

to believe what is not true. What is the purpose behind the deceitfulness of riches? The purpose is to convince us that our security is found in money and possessions, not in our Father. When we begin to believe that we are dependent on the world's economic system for our provision, we have been grossly misled!

Obviously, God usually provides for our needs through the earthly system of money. However, He is not dependent on it, and neither are we. We are dependent on Him. Knowing God as the source of every good and perfect gift is one of the great lessons of faith. In December 1986, one of our children learned this lesson in a big way!

Christmas List

As parents, Chuck and I never perpetuated the myth of Santa Claus with our children. To us, the miraculous birth of Jesus, the heavenly announcements and the humble worship of shepherds and kings were enough to fill the imagination of a child. This meant, of course, that our children knew we were the ones who bought the presents and put them under the tree, so they brought their Christmas lists to us. (In retrospect, perhaps we should have employed the Santa myth. At least then we could have blamed him when we could not get Rebekah a pony for Christmas!)

In December 1986, Chuck and I were living in a three-bedroom house in Houston with seventeen-year-old Joseph, two-year-old Rebekah, nine-month-old John Mark and Daniel. Of all the children, five-year-old Daniel was the one most excited about Christmas that year. He started his list right after Thanksgiving and updated it at least once a week. By the third week in December, the list had been revised so many times that it was barely readable. I had never seen a five-year-old get so stressed-out over a Christmas list.

One Sunday morning as the family dressed for church, Daniel walked into our bedroom, crying.

"What's the matter, son?" Chuck asked.

Daniel held out his hand. There, in the middle of his sweaty little palm, were the crumpled remains of his latest Christmas list. Chuck picked up the list and spread it open in his hands.

"I don't understand, honey," I said. "What happened to your list?"

Daniel was barely able to speak through the tears, but he managed to choke out the words, "I want something for Christmas that money can't buy!" Then sobbing, he collapsed on the floor of our bedroom.

Right there on the bedroom floor, Daniel prayed and asked the Lord Jesus into his heart. It was the best Christmas ever! Without a sermon or a Bible lesson, Daniel had heard the voice of God in the privacy of his own bedroom. Daniel allowed the Holy Spirit to expose the real need of his young heart that Christmas. That morning, God revealed Himself to Daniel as the perfect Christmas gift and delivered a little boy from the hand of mammon.

As we evaluate our relationship to money and possessions, let's consider another passage of Scripture vital to our understanding:

Do not lay up for yourselves treasures on earth, where moth and rust destroy and where thieves break in and steal; but lay up for yourselves treasures in heaven, where neither moth nor rust destroys and where thieves do not break in and steal. For where your treasure is, there your heart will be also.

Matthew 6:19–21

To maintain a right relationship to our "earthly treasures" while laying up our "treasures in heaven," we need to look at money and possessions through heaven's eyes.

A Rich Young Ruler

The gospels are full of significant encounters between Jesus and the people of Israel. Everywhere Jesus went, the multitudes flocked to Him for healing, ministry, teaching or just a touch. One day, a young man approached Jesus with a question:

> Now behold, one came and said to Him, "Good Teacher, what good thing shall I do that I may have eternal life?"
> So He said to him, "Why do you call Me good? No one is good but One, that is, God. But if you want to enter into life, keep the commandments."
> He said to Him, "Which ones?"
> Jesus said, "'You shall not murder,' 'You shall not commit adultery,' 'You shall not steal,' 'You shall not bear false witness,' 'Honor your father and your mother,' and, 'You shall love your neighbor as yourself.'"
> The young man said to Him, "All these things I have kept from my youth. What do I still lack?"
> Jesus said to him, "If you want to be perfect, go, sell what you have and give to the poor, and you will have treasure in heaven; and come, follow Me."
> But when the young man heard that saying, he went away sorrowful, for he had great possessions.
>
> Matthew 19:16–22

In spite of the young man's desire to do some "good thing" to earn eternal life, he could not let go of his earthly treasures. Jesus knew that this young man was too attached to his possessions to follow Him. The rich young ruler returned to his earthly treasures because that was where his heart lived. When Jesus looks at our hearts, does He see the same thing He saw in this young man? Do our earthly treasures hinder our ability to follow the Lord?

The rich young ruler's real problem was not his money and possessions. Instead, his problem was his *love for* and *attachment to* his money and possessions. In and of itself, money is not evil. On the contrary, in the right hands, money can accomplish much! Yet according to 1 Timothy 6:10, "The love of money is a root of all kinds of evil, for which some have strayed from the faith in their greediness, and pierced themselves through with many sorrows." The apostle Paul tells Timothy to give the rich in his care this warning:

> Command those who are rich in this present world not to be arrogant nor to put their hope in wealth, which is so uncertain, but to put their hope in God, who richly provides us with everything for our enjoyment. Command them to do good, to be rich in good deeds, and to be generous and willing to share. In this way they will lay up treasure for themselves as a firm foundation for the coming age, so that they may take hold of the life that is truly life.
>
> 1 Timothy 6:17–19, NIV

It is not our money and possessions that are the issue. Instead, it is our attitude toward our money and possessions that matter. Our hope is built on the Lord Jesus Christ, and our contentment must be centered in Him, not in worldly goods.

Godliness with Contentment

In Paul's letter to Timothy, just before the warning about the love of money, we read the following words:

Now godliness with contentment is great gain. For we brought nothing into this world, and it is certain we can carry nothing out. And having food and clothing, with these we shall be content. But those who desire to be rich fall into temptation and a snare, and into many foolish and harmful lusts which drown men in destruction and perdition.

1 Timothy 6:6–9

✱According to *Vine's Expository Dictionary of New Testament Words*, *godliness* "denotes that piety which, characterized by a Godward attitude, does that which is well-pleasing to Him" and is "embodied in, and communicated through, the truths of the faith concerning Christ." *Contentment* is "satisfaction with what one has." Consequently, godliness combined with contentment results in true wealth, or "great gain."[2]

As a five-year-old child consumed with his Christmas wish list, Daniel came face-to-face with his own lack of contentment. If the god of mammon can affect a child so profoundly, how much more can it impact adults who are choked by "the cares of this world" (Mark 4:19)?

Having a right relationship with money and possessions is all the more significant during times of economic uncertainty. Many people have seen their retirement funds dwindle, even disappear, over the last several months. Countless others have lost homes, jobs and health insurance. In spite of—or maybe because of—government reassurance, many Americans are plagued with doubt and fear about the future. These economic challenges put our faith to the test, and that is to be expected. The bottom line in the Christian life is, after all, faith, not our bank balance. We choose, day after day, whose report to believe. Will we believe the reports of Wall Street, Main Street and Pennsylvania Avenue? Or will we believe the report of the Lord?

It is possible for us to experience "godliness with contentment" even when the world's economic system is shaking. Let's examine 1 Timothy 6:6–9 a little more closely so we understand what Paul is saying:

- *"For we brought nothing into this world, and it is certain we can carry nothing out"* (verse 7). Hopefully, we all understand this statement! In spite of what the ancient Egyptians believed, nothing we accumulate in the way of material wealth will leave the earth with us. As Job said, "Naked I came from my mother's womb, and naked shall I return there. The LORD gave, and the LORD has taken away; blessed be the name of the LORD" (Job 1:21). The material blessings we receive from the Hand of God are intended for use here on earth. When we hoard those blessings out of fear (translate: lack of faith), we miss the opportunity to practice godliness. My dad—who has already moved to his heavenly address—taught me this. He was a generous man who loved the Lord with all his heart. His example as a selfless giver inspired Chuck and me early in our marriage to hold our earthly possessions loosely! We have never regretted it.
- *"And having food and clothing, with these we shall be content"* (verse 8). So far, our family has always been blessed with shelter and transportation in addition to food and clothing. Many times, all those items were stretched pretty thin. Joseph, Daniel and Rebekah remember the days when they had to save their meager allowances to buy something special once a month or when a trip to McDonald's was the highlight of the week. Our older children also remember the homegrown adventures in a rented farmhouse surrounded by seven acres. With five children and two adults sharing only fifteen hun-

dred square feet of house space, we spent a lot of time outdoors building forts, observing wildlife and picking wild blackberries. We were content because we treasured our time together and appreciated the goodness of God as He provided for our needs. We reduced, reused and recycled before it was fashionable—out of necessity! We never had money left over to save for the future, but we sure did enjoy the present! We chose as a family to believe that God was faithful, and that He would provide for our needs according to His riches in glory.

- *"But those who desire to be rich fall into temptation and a snare"* (verse 9). Just before Paul writes the statement, "For the love of money is a root of all kinds of evil" (verse 10), he tells Timothy that the desire to be rich leads into temptation and a trap. When the accumulation of wealth for wealth's sake becomes our desire, we are in serious danger of falling prey to the enemy and to the god of mammon. When we are caught in that trap, not only do we miss the rewards of simplicity, but we also risk joining the rich young ruler in the ultimate sorrow: choosing earthly wealth over the Lord Jesus Christ.

The apostle Paul understood the concept of "godliness with contentment" because he lived it. In Philippians 4:11–12 (NIV), he said, "For I have learned to be content whatever the circumstances. I know what it is to be in need, and I know what it is to have plenty. I have learned the secret of being content in any and every situation, whether well fed or hungry, whether living in plenty or in want." And what is the "secret of being content" that Paul had learned? "I can do everything through him who gives me strength" (Philippians 4:13, NIV).

Paul's secret was the Person of Jesus Christ. Later, in Hebrews 13:5–6, Paul encourages the reader to "let your conduct be without covetousness; be content with such things as you have. For He Himself has said, 'I will never leave you nor forsake you.' So we may boldly say: 'The LORD is my helper; I will not fear. What can man do to me?'"

Striving for wealth and being preoccupied with possessions both contradict faith. Simplification by faith requires us to renew our minds and agree with God about our relationship to money and possessions. When our relationship with them is grounded in faith, we can enter into the discipline of simplicity with freedom and joy. Unlike the rich young ruler, we can follow Jesus anywhere without fear of what will happen to our "stuff"!

When Presumption Overrules Faith

"Godliness with contentment" will also serve to protect or free us from the snare of credit card debt. Thirty years ago, before Chuck and I embarked on our first adventure involving the life of faith without a paycheck, the Lord clearly directed us to get rid of our credit cards. We did not know, at the time, that we were going to be living a very different sort of life within a few months. We thought the Lord just wanted us to streamline our financial situation. Instead, the Lord had some important lessons to teach us about presumption before Chuck gave up his salary!

My dictionary defines the word *presume* as:

- To take for granted as being true in the absence of proof to the contrary
- To venture without authority or permission; dare
- To take unwarranted advantage of something; go beyond the proper limits

97

Presumption is the "behavior or attitude that is boldly arrogant or offensive; effrontery," or "the act of presuming or accepting as true."[3]

For the believer, out-of-control credit card debt is evidence of presumption. Obviously, I am not referring to using a credit card for convenience or for purchases that require that method of payment. I am referring to the snare connected to credit card use. When we do not exercise self-control or faith, we can quickly lose track of just how much money we have spent simply because it is so easy to swipe the card instead of write the check or use the debit card.

By its very nature, credit card spending creates a mindset of presumption because we are spending what we do not have or we are borrowing from what is to come. And, let's be honest—when we borrow from what is to come, we are presuming that God has agreed to pay for something before we even check in with Him!

If we look at the definition of *presume* from the perspective of money, we arrive at a slightly altered meaning:

- To take for granted that there is money in the bank to pay for that credit card purchase when the bank balance says something to the contrary
- To venture out and buy something with the credit card when the Holy Spirit has not given the go-ahead (to disobey!)
- To take advantage of the credit card's convenience to go beyond our monthly limit

Remember, the god of mammon does not want us to live free from presumption or from unnecessary debt. He wants to ensnare us in a vicious cycle of impulsive purchases, excessive interest rates and financial chaos. But credit card abuse has another effect on our lives, as well. According to a 2000 study published in the journal *Social Science & Medicine*, "People with a high ratio of credit card debt to income were in worse physical health than those with less debt." Our Father, on the other hand, wants us to experience the freedom and joy of "godliness with contentment."[4]

Back in 1979, when the Lord told Chuck and me to stop using the credit card for anything, that was actually not too difficult for us. There was no online shopping in 1979; Chuck only traveled for work and the company paid for everything; and we could easily write checks or pay cash for anything we needed. Even so, we had to adjust our habits to reflect this new direction from the Lord. We had to apply principles of faith to our money and leave presumption behind where money was concerned.

What does credit card spending have to do with simplicity? For starters, when we apply faith principles to credit card spending, we are much less likely to fall into impulse buying. Fewer impulse purchases means less "stuff" we have to store when we get home. When we stop operating in presumption concerning credit card purchases, we can hear God much more clearly about what we actually *need* as opposed to what we *want*. This results in an inner environment of peace, which naturally flows outward.

Rich toward God

When we embrace a skewed concept of money and possessions, we have a tendency to hang on to anything with potential value. Like the rich man with the fertile fields and abundant crops, we might be inclined to build bigger barns instead of clearing out our excess. But one of the rewards of simplification is the freedom from clutter we can all enjoy!

99

Once we have been set free from the deceitfulness of riches and the desire for other things, the discipline of simplicity becomes second nature.

When I look at my life and my home, I want to be able to say that I am rich toward God. I do not want to look around and feel overwhelmed by the things I have accumulated out of some empty desire to lay up earthly treasure. My goal as a wife, mother, friend and child of the King is to enjoy every good and pleasant thing God has provided for this life without compromising the life to come. This requires vigilance, because the enemy will use every opportunity to undermine our faith and convince us that mammon is a more reliable provider than the Lord Jesus Christ.

As we allow the Lord to adjust our attitude toward money and possessions, let's be encouraged by this word from Matthew 6:31–33:

> Therefore do not worry, saying, "What shall we eat?" or "What shall we drink?" or "What shall we wear?" For after all these things the Gentiles seek. For your heavenly Father knows that you need all these things. But seek first the kingdom of God and His righteousness, and all these things shall be added to you.

When we seek God's Kingdom and His righteousness *before* we seek all those other things we need (or want), we operate in a level of faith that pleases God. And knowing Him as our provider and our source brings many rewards far beyond worldly wealth. As Hebrews 11:6 reminds us: "But without faith it is impossible to please Him, for he who comes to God must believe that He is, and that He is a rewarder of those who diligently seek Him."

7

Practicing Simplicity

Many years ago, I asked our family doctor this question: "Why do doctors call what they do *practicing medicine?*"

Without hesitation, he answered, "Because we *are* practicing. We continue learning and perfecting what we do. If a doctor gets to the point where he thinks he knows everything there is to know about the human body and why it does whatever it does, he ceases to learn. We are constantly practicing the skills we need to help our patients."

We need the same attitude as we approach the spiritual discipline of simplicity. Even after learning all we can about why, how, when and where to simplify our lives, we still have to put all of the principles into practice, little by little. If we attempt to simplify every aspect of our lives—spiritual, mental and physical—all at once, it will overwhelm us. It is important that we enter into every phase of simplification with patience, by faith, so that we know we are operating by the Spirit rather than by the flesh. Only then will we experience the rewards of simplicity.

In this book, Chuck and I share several principles about simplification and give some guidelines for working toward it. Before we launch into some very specific strategies for achieving simplicity, let's quickly review what I have covered so far. In chapter 1, I shared three keys I have found essential to my own pursuit of simplification:

1. Faith—Let the Holy Spirit be your guide in every act of simplification, from cleaning out your closets to eliminating stressful commitments in your life. Guard against simplifying some aspect of your life, home or work just because you do not like it. Plenty of things, activities and even people consume our time and complicate our lives. "Not liking" something—or someone—is not why we eliminate them from our lives. Let the Holy Spirit be your guide as you evaluate your circumstances.

2. Focus—Once the Holy Spirit shows you something that needs simplification, either through elimination or adjustment, seek His guidance for focus. This key involves directing your attention to the task at hand. Focus might include purposefully setting aside time from your normal routine to give the task your undivided attention. It is sometimes necessary to behave like my son John Mark did when he was learning to play the guitar!

3. Function—This is when you put your faith and focus into action. For example, suppose I determine that mowing my own lawn is consuming too much of my time. The Holy Spirit tells me to simplify that task by finding someone else to do the job for me, so my next

step is to ask the Lord to show me whom He wants to mow my lawn. The answer might be obvious (the kid down the street), but then, it might not be! Even function is an act of faith.

I often find that the boundaries between these three keys get blurred. Some evaluations proceed from faith to function in a moment. When that happens, I just flow with it. I know—and so will you—when the simplification is by the Spirit or by the flesh. Trust your relationship with the Father. He cares about the details of your life more than you know!

I have also shared portions of the following definitions already, but they dovetail so well with this chapter's theme that I want to be sure they are fresh in our minds:

Simple:
- Free from guile—innocent
- Free from vanity—modest
- Free from ostentation or display
- Of humble origin or modest position

Simplify:
- To make simple or simpler
- To reduce to basic essentials
- To diminish in scope or complexity—streamline
- To make more intelligible—clarify

Remember, simplicity is not easy. Many times, doing the simple thing *by faith* is more difficult than maintaining the way we are used to operating in a complex world. Whenever I begin to simplify anything, I remind myself of this quote from well-known economist and statistician E. F. Schumacher:

103

"Any intelligent fool can make things bigger, more complex, and more violent. It takes a touch of genius—and a lot of courage—to move in the opposite direction."[1] So, press into your new role as a courageous genius and practice simplicity by faith!

In earlier chapters, I also shared several other aspects of simplification. One was fasting for simplification—not necessarily from food, though that can be beneficial. We talked about fasting from electronic media and entertainment, which tend to complicate and crowd our lives more than ever before. We talked about simplicity and the law of love, which boils down to putting people before things or our own activities. Simplifying our schedule to accommodate others expresses love as nothing else can.

I also have learned so much about the importance of the Sabbath as I have begun to simplify my life. I shared those insights in chapter 5, along with the importance of creation's role in refreshing us. In chapter 6 we discussed our relationship to money and possessions. Striving for wealth and being preoccupied with possessions both contradict faith, whereas knowing God is our Source is one of the great lessons of faith. Godliness with contentment and being rich toward God are vital to simplification.

Since the first key to simplicity is faith, and anxiety wars against our faith, it is essential to understand how the world, the flesh and the devil use anxiety to propagate chaos and confusion in our lives. In his chapters just ahead, Chuck will expose anxiety for what it really is and provide us with vital information for setting our hearts and minds free from anxiety's snares. Like Martha, many of us are subject to worry and trouble. Because my husband, Chuck, has so much more experience with the pitfalls of anxiety, he will be our guide in dealing with that area.

As believers in the Lord Jesus Christ, we are a people of faith. Because of this fact, our enemy uses every possible advantage to undermine that faith and cripple us with unbelief. The everyday stress of life clutters our hearts and minds and creates the perfect environment for anxiety to thrive. But remember what Jesus said to us in John 16:33: "In the world you will have tribulation; but be of good cheer, I have overcome the world." As we will see in Chuck's chapters, choosing to simplify *by faith* is one of the weapons we can use against the crippling effects of anxiety.

Where Do We Start?

That is a taste of where we have been and where we are going, but in the rest of this chapter, I want to examine with you other practical, real-life strategies for simplification relating to these, and other, areas of modern life.

Before embarking further on any course of simplification in your own home and life, however, please consider this: If you share your life with others, proceed in love. Whenever we choose to simplify any area of life, it can—and often does—affect those around us. Do not assume that your spouse, your children, your extended family and your friends are convinced that simplification is of any value. For example, just because I think we have too many pictures and knickknacks in our house does not give me the right to load them up in boxes and head to a resale shop. My husband enjoys collecting art and artifacts, and I love him enough to leave his collections alone. If he chooses to simplify our décor, however, I will be right there with the boxes and bubble wrap to help him unclutter!

Another factor to consider is that many of us have been obsessed with hoarding clutter. Regardless of our motivation for hanging on to useless (or outdated, impractical and un-necessary) stuff, we do not have to continue cluttering our homes, offices or lives with things that inhibit our ability to live according to God's order and purpose for us. If hoarding is—or has been—an issue for you, here are a few suggestions for overcoming that tendency:

- *Surrender Sentimentality.* Do not throw away the fam-ily photos or the baby books, but do you really need the last ten years' worth of birthday and Christmas cards? Consider the storage requirements for some of the nostalgia, and clean out accordingly.
- *Share the Surplus.* That extra blender you have been keeping just in case your current one bites the dust? Someone you know could be enjoying the benefits while you wait for your old one to die! Let your surplus be someone else's answer to prayer.
- *Stuff In, Stuff Out.* Anytime you buy a new shirt, dress, pair of shoes, set of towels, anything—let go of some-thing you already have. My husband is really good at this. If he buys two new shirts, he takes at least that many to someone at the office (or elsewhere) who will gladly accept his gently worn gift.
- *Say, "So Long" to Someday.* That broken appliance, frame or knickknack you have been meaning to fix for the last two years needs to go. If you have not managed to get it fixed yet, you probably never will. Donate it—today—to someone who may be able to fix it or use the parts. Say good-bye to that stash of "maybe I can fix this" items out in the garage. This applies to just about anything you have been meaning to mend or repair for a while. Besides freeing up space, you will avoid the guilt you experience every time you see the item.

Starting from the Inside Out

The contemporary minimalist advocate D. H. Mondfleur once said, "Eliminate physical clutter. More importantly, eliminate spiritual clutter."[2] We have spent a good bit of time dealing with spiritual clutter already, so now it is time to look at some other areas of our lives.

I do not know about you, but it has always been difficult for me to effectively separate the physical from the spiritual in my own life. In other words, when my physical environment or condition is cluttered, that is usually a good indication that something is amiss in my spiritual environment, as well. I can temporarily store spiritual clutter in soulish closets and cabinets until a more convenient time, a time when I can effectively and honestly clean my spiritual house. In the same way, I can hide the true condition of my home behind closet and cabinet doors so that no one knows how out-of-control my housekeeping has become—that is, until someone unwittingly opens the hall closet and has to dig his way out of the avalanche. For this reason, I always start the task of uncluttering (simplifying) by cleaning out my home's hidden storage areas. There are three reasons for this strategy:

1. The out-of-sight, out-of-mind problem. Many times, when we do not know what to do with something, we just stash it in a closet, cabinet or drawer. Over time, because we did not store that particular item based on any logical storage system, we forget where in the world we put it. Regularly cleaning out those hidden places unearths either trash or treasure. Remember what 1 Corinthians 4:5 says: "Therefore judge nothing before the time, until the Lord comes, who will both bring to light the hidden things of darkness and reveal the counsels of the hearts." Of course, we do not have

the mysteries of God hidden in our closets, but you get the idea!

2. Perhaps you, your parents or even your grandparents said this at one time or another: "A place for everything and everything in its place." If you do not know what you have hidden in your closets, cabinets and drawers, how do you know if everything *is* in its place to start with? First Corinthians 14:40 says, "Let all things be done decently and in order." Again, we are talking about "stuff," not tongues and prophecy, but the sentiment applies. When there is "a place for everything and everything in its place," we save valuable time and resources by not hunting for something or having to replace it.

3. When we clean out and reorganize closets, cabinets and drawers, we multiply our available storage space for those things we really need to keep. As we create this new space out of the clutter, we will have room for those things that have been out in the open for want of concealed storage.

The most basic strategy for cleaning out a home's storage and other areas involves the use of a "three-box system." This system employs three boxes labeled "Keep," "Give/Sell," and "Toss." As you sift through the contents of your home's hidden storage areas, every out-of-place, unwanted or unnecessary item will go into one of those boxes. I also add a fourth box labeled "Decide Later." That box is for those obscure items I discover that look important, but I just do not know why! Usually, I have to ask my kids about the "Decide Later" items. Many times, they are able to identify the items as part of a discarded remote control, battery charger or video game system. Every once in a while, however, some precious missing treasure turns up in the "Decide Later" box, which is why I use it!

Be prepared to feel overwhelmed when you start this process. It can be daunting. That is why I encourage you to tackle this job in small increments. Unless you are highly motivated and have a lot of time, you will probably want to start with one room, maybe even one closet, at a time. If you have a large family, I definitely recommend pacing yourself. And parents, remember to include your children when you start on their bedrooms. Once, while cleaning out Daniel's room, I discarded a toy that I did not think he cared about. When he discovered my treachery, he was very sad to learn that I had thrown away something with significant sentimental value. I learned my lesson.

While you do need to tread softly in your roommate's, children's or spouse's storage areas, your own territory is fair game. Be brutal, especially in your clothes closet (or in some cases, clothes *closets*) and dressers. For many of us, this really requires some faith. Seriously, though, if we have not worn something in over a year (or, at the most, two years) are we really ever going to wear it? Granted, there are some exceptions, especially in the realm of formal wear, seasonal garments or clothing with sentimental value. But that suit with the padded shoulders from the 1980s that does not even fit? Really?

As far as clothes are concerned, less is more in my opinion. Comfort is more important to me than appearance, but if I find something that is comfortable *and* attractive, I will wear it out. I do not have a lavish walk-in closet, so space is at a premium. I do have access to another closet in the house where I can hang my winter clothes during the long, wonderful Texas summers, so that helps. If you do not have that option, it is even more important to evaluate your closet's contents honestly and with an open mind. Remember, this is an exercise in faith. Let the Holy Spirit guide you. Many times, the Lord has placed His hand on a particular garment and shown me exactly whom to give it to. Then I enjoy the double benefit of blessing someone else *and* having more space.

As you make your way from closet to closet and room to room, your three (or four) boxes will start filling up. The "Toss" box is easy to deal with—discard the contents. If you recycle (and we all should), separate the recyclables first. If some items are still usable, start a box in the garage for the Salvation Army or other local charity. Everything else goes to the curb!

The "Keep" box requires a little more effort. Remember "a place for everything and everything in its place"? Each item in the "Keep" box needs a new home. This is where logic comes in to play. If, for example, you found a board game in your linen closet, that is not a logical place for it! You probably have a place for games already, so take it there. If not, dedicate a shelf somewhere in your newly liberated cabinets for all your board games. Deciding how often you use an item will help you determine how accessible each item or group of items should be. We use our board games regularly, so we keep them all on a shelf in the hall closet. Christmas decorations, on the other hand, are only used once a year, so they go out to the garage shelves. If you live in a cooler climate, you are probably able to use your attic or basement for out-of-season storage.

The "Keep" box will most likely contain several items belonging to other members of your household. Encourage family members to follow your lead. Help your children and your spouse develop logical strategies for storing their belongings. This is a skill the kids will use for the rest of their lives. Once, when Ethan and I were cleaning out his closets, he got so overwhelmed by all of his stuff that he wanted to throw it all away rather than develop a logical system of storage. It took me a while to convince him that the task was doable, but we finally turned his chaotic space into a more simplified, organized one. Now, if I can just convince him to maintain it!

When you get to the "Give/Sell" box, you have a lot of options. Start with the items that you know you want to give to friends, family, church members or neighbors. Sack them up, label them and put them in the car. Get them out of the house before you change your mind and decide you might need them someday.

Some items in your box may be worth the time and effort to sell. In these days of Craigslist and eBay, it is easier than ever to find buyers for all kinds of things. Another option is your local resale shop. Still another option is the old standby, the garage sale. I have to confess, every time I have a garage sale, I swear I will never do it again. It is a lot of work. But it can be worth the effort, especially if you can get your kids to help. If you do choose the garage sale option, promise yourself that you will *not* bring anything left after the sale back into the house. Box it up and take it to the Salvation Army.

Depending on the size of your home and family and how much time you can dedicate to the job, this first step of simplifying can take anywhere from a day to a year! Do not get overwhelmed and lose heart. It took a while for your hidden storage places to get so cluttered and unorganized; it will take some time to unclutter and organize them. Simplifying and cleaning out is a lot like losing weight: It takes a while to gain twenty pounds—it will take a while to lose it, too!

Creating an Uncluttered Environment

Now that we have cleaned out the hidden storage places in our homes, it is time to direct our attention to the visible storage places. When bookshelves, tabletops, walls and counters are cluttered with decorative—or even functional—objects, our lives feel more cluttered, as well. I have found that clutter causes several problems:

- Dusting furniture is a much bigger chore when every surface is cluttered.
- Too many knickknacks cause sensory overload. When every available surface is occupied with a decorative item, I do not know what to look at first!
- A cluttered environment makes it much more difficult to find what we need when we need it.

Add to the decorative clutter the everyday accumulation of "stuff" coming in from the outside world, and we have a recipe for chaos! How, then, do we find a balance between a functional, organized environment and an aesthetically pleasing one? I employ several strategies for coping with decorative clutter. Let's consider a few of them:

- The Purging Strategy—I am a big fan of this one, but not everyone can embrace it. This strategy involves going through every room with a box and collecting every knickknack, picture and doodad that you do not absolutely love. I admit, "absolutely love" is a bit of hyperbole. What I want to convey is this: Any decorative item that has no intrinsic or artistic value *to you or a family member* needs to go in the box. You will not miss it when you take it to the resale shop, add it to your garage sale stack or give it to the Salvation Army.

112

- The Cycle Strategy—This one is much less drastic, but still effective. When you cycle your decorative objects, you go through the house with a box and pull *at least* 25 percent of the knickknacks, pictures and doodads off the shelves and place them in the box. Once you get started, you might increase that 25 percent to 50 percent, depending on how much you like the less cluttered environment. Then you take the box to one of your newly liberated closets or cabinets and store it for a few weeks. At the end of that time, if you do not miss the items you boxed up, you might consider permanently removing those items from your home. Otherwise, you can bring the box back out in a few months and trade out the remaining knickknacks for the ones in the box. This strategy unclutters and allows you to keep your decorative items without purging. It also adds variety to your décor without added expense.

- The Combination Strategy—As the name implies, this is a combination of purging and cycling. This involves going through the house with two boxes: one for cycling and one for discarding. This strategy is a good solution for someone who wants to get serious about clutter without making a final commitment about everything. Your goal would be to eliminate surface clutter by *at least* 50 percent.

It is amazing how much a cluttered household can affect our sense of peace and comfort. Clutter creates an atmosphere of confusion and unrest, both of which war against the environment we all really want—and need—in our homes. So, choose your strategy and liberate yourself from unnecessary clutter!

Taming Mail Clutter

I just came in from the mailbox, which was full with just one day's delivery. Out of all the mail I brought into the house, only two envelopes required any sort of attention: the gas bill and a birthday card. The rest of the stack included several catalogs (for things I do not need), solicitations for donations to charitable organizations and offers of new credit cards. After shredding the credit card offers, I put all but the gas bill and the birthday card in the recycle bin. Within just a few days, my recycle bin will be full of catalogs and junk mail. (I am so thankful for curbside recycling; it has truly helped simplify my life.)

Even after cleaning out hidden storage areas and eliminating surface clutter in our homes, the problem of incoming clutter can get out of control in a heartbeat if we do not have a plan for managing it. For this reason, it is worthwhile to choose *one place in your home* for dealing with mail and incoming paperwork. Here is what I suggest:

- Create a mail center. Whether it is the kitchen table or a desk in your home office, all incoming paperwork needs to go to that spot! If possible, include the following items at this mail center: an inbox, a waste/recycling bin, a small filing system (like an accordion folder) and something in which to store envelopes, stamps, the checkbook, pens, stapler and paper clips.

- All incoming mail or other paperwork goes directly to the inbox. That way the catalogs, junk mail and bills do not get scattered all over the kitchen counter or entry table. If possible, immediately sort the mail. Toss the junk and catalogs into the recycling bin. Then all you will have left will be mail that requires your attention.

- Once a week (at least), sit down with your inbox and take care of everything in it. If something in the stack will require more than a few minutes of your attention, place it in the small filing system for later attention. Do not put it back in the inbox.

- Pay the bills promptly. If you use online banking, take advantage of your bank's bill pay service. (Personally, I love not having to write checks and mail payments.) Otherwise, write that check, put a stamp on it and do not forget to mail it!

- If any of the paperwork in your inbox concerns upcoming appointments, parties or other commitments, record that information on your calendar or in your organizer (paper or electronic). You might also want to explore the option of an online calendar, such as Google Calendar.

- File away! Once you have paid a bill or taken appropriate action concerning each item in the inbox, file it or throw it away. Do not start a new stack or put anything back into the inbox. Keep your filing system simple, too, or you will find it hard to maintain.

If you have not set up an organized method for dealing with incoming paper, it may take a while to teach yourself some new tricks. But do not give up! It is worth the effort, and before long, this system (or one like it) will become a natural part of your household routine.

If you find your mailbox inundated with unsolicited catalogs, there is help online. Catalog Choice is a free service that allows you to let catalog companies know whether you actually want to receive their publications. According to their website, "The mission of Catalog Choice is to reduce the number of repeat and unwanted catalog mailings, and to promote the adoption of sustainable industry best practices. We aim to accomplish this by freely providing the Catalog Choice Mail Preference Service to both consumers and businesses. Consumers can indicate their mail preference for catalogs, and sign up for Email news, and businesses can receive the lists in a secure manner so that they can efficiently honor the requests."[3]

I have been using the Catalog Choice service for several years now. Not every catalog business honors the requests from the website, but many do. It has at least put a dent in the number of catalogs clogging my mailbox and filling my recycling bin.

Streamlining the Calendar

Uncluttering our calendars can be an even bigger challenge than cleaning out our closets, especially for families with busy children. In chapter 4, "Simplicity and the Law of Love," I outlined the following strategy for evaluating your use of time and energy:

- List your top priorities. What is most important to you? What (or whom) do you value most?
- List your commitments. Consider everything, including work, church, household, family, children's extracurricular activities, hobbies, freelance work, even leisure time. Which of these commitments do you value most? Which of these fit into the top priorities you have already listed?
- Account for your time. How do you spend your waking hours? From the time you get up until the time you go to sleep, what are you doing with your time? Are you using any of your time for your top priorities?

If you completed this exercise while reading chapter 4, then you already know the answers to the following questions regarding each time commitment on your calendar. If you did not yet complete the exercise and answer the questions, do so now.

- Does this add meaning/value to my life?
- How important is this to me?
- Does this conflict with or enhance my priorities?
- Could I eliminate this from my life?

If you have children, help them use these questions to evaluate their schedules. While many children thrive on extra-curricular activities, others experience stress-related symptoms when their schedules do not allow for enough play or leisure time. As parents, we are responsible to protect our children from "too much, too soon." On the other hand, we can also use these questions to help our children recognize that they spend way too much time online or in front of the television!

Simplify, One Day at a Time

We are all familiar with the saying, "Anything worth doing is worth doing well." That certainly applies to the practice of simplicity. While we could rush through the motions of simplifying and just address the external aspects of simplicity, we will all benefit from a patient, thoughtful approach—a disciplined approach. Galatians 6:9 says, "Let us not become weary in doing good, for at the proper time we will reap a harvest if we do not give up" (NIV). With practice, we can all reap the rewards of simplicity.

As we embark on the bold adventure of ridding our homes—and our lives—of clutter, let's keep our sense of

117

humor intact. Here is a little poem I wrote (okay, I am no Robert Frost!) for the occasion:

"Clutter Came Calling"

Clutter came calling, with baggage in hand,
To scatter his chaos all over the land.
His plan was quite simple: convince everyone
That "more" is much better and frantic means "fun."
So clutter got busy (it didn't take long)
And soon the whole kingdom was singing his song:
"More, we want more," so that's what they got,
But now they need storage for all that they bought!

PART 2

Chuck Speaks on SIMPLIFYING Life by Overcoming Anxiety

8

Simplicity or Anxiety?

One Must Choose!

A s you saw earlier, when Pam related the discussion she and I had about hand raising in church, I have had my moments of *simple*, uncluttered *faith*. Through the years, the Word of God has become the ultimate authority in my life, and our authority relationships are key to our faith. When an authority in my life develops a premise and I know the principle is correct, I try to do what I am supposed to do as a result. God is my authority, so I try to think as He thinks and do what His Word says. It is that simple! The way we think about and respond to the object of our faith is one determi nant of how simple—or how complex—our lives will be.

We are living in incredible, changing times. Because I am a prophetic voice in the Body of Christ, my job is to share what the Lord is saying for comfort, encouragement, warning and direction. Recently, I was seeking the Lord for His word for the year ahead. I had heard Him impress several things on my heart, and I was gaining insights from Scripture when Pam called to share a dream with me.

Dream revelation is one of the key ways the Spirit of God speaks to us. In my book *When God Speaks*, I share the following about dreams:

> A dream is a release of revelation (whether natural or spiritual) that comes at a time when your body is at peace and you are settled. Sometimes this is the only way God can communicate with us because our soul is quiet enough for the Lord to speak deeply into our spirit man. A dream is like a snapshot of something you are able to relate to in picture form. Ecclesiastes 5:3 tells us that a dream comes when there are many cares. They can either be a subconscious response to the circumstances of our lives, or the Holy Spirit communicating to us. As Jane Hamon states in her book, *Dreams and Visions*, "Dreams are formed in the subconscious mind of a man or woman based on images and symbols which are unique to the individual, depending on his or her background, experience and current life circumstances. Dreams can communicate to us truth about ourselves—or others—which our conscious mind may have failed to acknowledge."
>
> Dreams can originate strictly within the natural mind or can be given as messages from God's Spirit and received within the mind of man. . . . If we compare the communication of the Spirit of the Lord through dreams to other methods of divine communication mentioned in Scripture—prophecy, a word of knowledge, etc.—the primary difference is that dreams are given first to our subconscious minds before being perceived by our conscious minds.[1]

Whenever I am at home in Denton on Tuesdays, I make it a priority to lead early morning intercessory prayer at Glory of Zion International Ministries. Pam is not a "crack-of-dawn" person, so she usually waves good-bye from bed and goes back to sleep as soon as I leave the house at 5:30. On this particular Tuesday morning, Pam had a dream when she went back to sleep. Later that morning, she called to relate it to me:

I woke up slowly this morning to the sound of singing birds, and it was as though I were walking through a curtain that divided the dream world from the waking world. As I lay there, I began remembering my dream: I was with a group of travelers, none of whom I recognized, but I knew they were important to me. We were told we had to take a trip, but we had no luggage, tickets or itinerary. We were standing in a hallway similar to one you might see in an airport, waiting for our departure. Suddenly, this strong wind began to blow down the hallway (wind tunnel) and push us toward the open end of the corridor. As we got closer to the end of the corridor, some kind of portal opened up, but it wasn't like what you see in the science fiction show *Stargate*! The light was warm, and as we entered the portal area, we were disembodied and transported to another place. Strangely, the other place didn't look any different than the place we had just been. However, it was not the same place. We were inside a building, made mostly of glass (like the Pennzoil Place in Houston, Texas).

We all knew we had to fly to get where we needed to go. None of us knew how to fly, but we just took off and started flying around the lobby. The people in the lobby were amazed and started reaching for us, saying they wanted to fly, too. We knew we needed more momentum to get where we needed to be, so we landed softly, turned around and got a running start before launching ourselves from a mini-trampoline in the café area of the lobby.

Instantly we were outside the building, in a country setting, and we knew our mission: *Rescue a captive in the nearby village and bring him/her back with us.* The mission itself is still vague, but I remember what happened when we were ready to return. One of the villagers wanted to go with us but knew it wasn't possible, so he gave each of us a tiny jewel case. Mine was a small, gold case encrusted with pearls. Inside the case were bits and pieces of broken jewelry—pearls, gold beads, crystals. Each case had a word on it. The word on the outside of mine was *Simplify*. We thanked the one who gave us the gifts, then turned to launch back into the sky for the return trip.

That's when the birds woke me up.

Pam's dream contained several key portions of revelation embedded within its contents. Here are some key points that will benefit you in the days ahead as you seek to simplify your life:

- We will gain entryway into new fields that we have never before had opportunity to enter.
- We must be ready to travel without any "baggage." Therefore, this is a time of lightening our load.
- We can rise up, but once we do, we must gain momentum and not stop until we reach our destination.
- There are many missions ahead for those of us who are called for "such a time as this" (see Esther 4:14).
- We must stay focused only on our assigned mission and not allow emotional connections to attach themselves to us.
- With the changing times and the complexities of society, we could easily become overwhelmed about how we will accomplish God's call and destiny for our lives.
- We need to receive the gift of *simplification*. If we simplify now, we will prosper in days ahead.

The word of the Lord was *simplify*. This dream has accelerated Pam and me on the journey that you are now entering with us as you read this book.

Restoring Simplicity

In chapter 1, Pam showed amazing insight when she wrote, "We just knew that God had momentarily stripped us down to the bare necessities so that He could bless us. Simplicity is a place of blessing for believers, whether we enter into it by accident or design. When we move by faith, with focus, into the function of simplicity, blessings abound!"

Oh my, what a statement Pam makes! How awesome it sounds to the ear. Actually, it is simple to hear this statement, and if we would practice it on every occasion and in every circumstance, we would live in joy and freedom. But alas, we are a complex people with many thoughts of our own, and hearing is one thing, doing is another. However, our development is an ongoing journey. Let me take you on my journey out of anxiety and into simplicity. How would the Lord begin a process to take me from worry and fear to faith and obedience? Read on and watch His grace at work.

Let me begin by saying *I was a worrier.* I do not think I was born a worrier, but I believe the turn of events in our family life developed this frictional emotion in me at an early age. By the time I was in fourth grade, I had an ulcer and I was taking Valium. Yes, Valium! Our family life at home had begun to degenerate and I was a high achiever in school, so I tried to achieve as a stress reliever. My extended family had always met together to work the land we owned and have large barbeques and dinners on the grounds. Therefore, family gatherings and eating were part of my early development. But then that portion of my life began deteriorating, and by the time I reached sixteen years of age, family as I had known it had been completely destroyed and rearranged.

Family was God's original plan for society. Family was the first war unit in the earth. My family was destroyed; apparently we were a bloodline and generation in utter defeat. Because dangerous, dysfunctional events involving gambling, alcoholism, violence and corruption ran rampant in my family, my peaceful childhood became one of chaos and constant alertness. This caused full-blown anxiety in my emotional being.

In survival mode, I developed the ability to always anticipate every issue that could arise and prepare myself for the worst-case scenario. In most situations, before these stressful events would happen, I would lie awake thinking of what could happen, how it could happen and what my response should be when it occurred. And trust me—the scenario usually materialized just the way I had imagined, and then I felt prepared to respond.

God works all things to good for those who love Him. Knowing that, I have to say that my ability to perceive what might lie ahead was part of the prophetic gifting that would eventually develop and mature in me. But for many years, the gift was just a way for me to foresee danger and anxiously wait for "the next shoe to drop," the next big brawl or the next escape I would need to make from a dangerous environment.

Anxiety Develops and Progresses

Anxiety is progressive. Anxiety moves into fear. Fear develops into control. The fear of losing control eventually becomes panic. Panic then becomes trauma. Your present becomes your past, which is called post-traumatic stress syndrome. It is also called post-traumatic stress disorder, or PTSD. According to Jonathan Davidson and Henry Dreher in *The Anxiety Book*, PTSD has three key sets of symptoms:

1. You constantly relive the trauma in the form of recurring memories, flashbacks or nightmares (known as "reexperiencing" or "intrusive" symptoms);
2. You avoid feelings about the trauma, or situations that trigger those feelings, by becoming numb or detached (referred to as "avoidance" and "numbing" symptoms);
3. You feel agitated, irritable and quick off the trigger; have trouble concentrating or sleeping; are easily startled; and are on a state of "high alert" all the time (called "hyperarousal" symptoms).[2]

I guess you could say I became an *"on high alert"* individual. All stability ended and disaster occurred when my dad died a premature, violent death. I was sixteen at the time, and his death posed many more new problems for me. The responsibility of taking care of the land, having a younger brother and sister and the necessity of continuing to be a high achiever produced more internal friction in me. Being called on to be a provider added another dimension to my already stressed-out life. I had little understanding, guidance or counseling to help me with this huge responsibility, and by the time I was eighteen, I just wanted to escape. However, high achievers usually see no way to escape because they are too responsible to run. Therefore, their bombarding thought is *How will I make it through this crisis?* Life itself becomes a crisis!

All you can seem to do in such a situation is live life on high alert. You cannot really rest, because as the famous line says, "Tomorrow is another day"—and you know tomorrow will surely add more responsibilities and more problems to the ones from the preceding day. Before you know it, nothing is simple, and you have developed a very complex lifestyle of survival.

You experience some good moments, but no actual rest. You want to take time to smell the roses, but you think that must be put off for another day. Yes, the Lord can work this out. He can send help. He will be there for you. However, you really do not take the time nor a peaceful moment to seek that help because you are too occupied with planning the next hour and thinking through what things could be like tomorrow. Yet you really do not call your condition *anxiety* or recognize it as such. The condition just becomes who you are all the time and overtakes the personality that God destined you to exhibit in life.

Be Anxious for Nothing? Sure Thing!

When trauma and the need to survive are a constant part of your life, anxiety no longer is an occasional occurrence in your day or a fleeting emotional readjustment. Worrying is something you just do all the time. Being anxious is what you become, who you are. But out of my own experience, I want to make a positive faith statement: You *can* recover and become functional again. This is not easy, but you can do it. Repeat after me: *I think I can . . . I think I can!* Philippians 4:4–9 (CJB) states,

> Rejoice in union with the Lord always! I will say it again: rejoice! Let everyone see how reasonable and gentle you are. The Lord is near! Don't worry about anything; on the contrary, make your requests known to God by prayer and petition, with thanksgiving. Then God's shalom, passing all understanding, will keep your hearts and minds safe in union with the Messiah Yeshua. In conclusion, brothers, focus your thoughts on what is true, noble, righteous, pure, lovable or admirable, on some virtue or on something praiseworthy. Keep doing what you have learned and received from me, what you have heard and seen me doing; then the God who gives shalom will be with you.

The New Living Translation says to "always be full of joy" and "tell God what you need, and thank him for all he has done" (verses 4, 6). If ever there was a passage of Scripture that I found myself warring against through the years, the above promise, that *shalom* would be with me, would be that Scripture. People with severe anxiety deny their condition. First, you rationalize what you feel. You then justify why you should be nervous or prone to worry. After all, you have the world around you (and much of the outside world) resting on your shoulders. You pretend that severe anxiety is not a normal part of your life, when in reality you awaken with one set of thoughts that create anxiety and go to bed worrying about a whole new set of thoughts full of scenarios depicting all the things that could go wrong. You then begin to believe that everyone must live like this, and you become very cynical toward those who seem happy and are enjoying life. Life seems so simple for them, whereas you seem to run into complications at every turn.

The most difficult issue is admitting that what you consider right and true about how best to live, as written in Scripture, you really do not put into practice. I will not say that you do not believe, but I will comment that one does not always *do* what one believes. Demons believe, but that obviously does not mean they live the way the Word says! You *can* change your anxious state, though, by doing what the Word says about it. God's children obey and adhere to every word from His mouth, and their lives are a demonstration of His wisdom. This is what produces our testimony. And our testimony overcomes.

In *The Anxiety Book*, Davidson and Dreher also write,

Recovering from anxiety requires real commitment, but it is a liberating process that restores meaning and pleasure to your life. . . . Know that you can transform your life from a daily battle with anxious preoccupations, paralyzing fears, and compulsive behaviors to a state of greater peace, creativity, energy, and joy.[3]

For a long time, I worried. I did not praise. I was thankful for my present but not for my past. Therefore, I feared what the future would bring. In certain situations it is utterly normal to have concerns—but it is never normal to worry incessantly over routine work assignments, what others think about your accomplishments, how you look or the ups and downs of your bank account. And then of course, there is your kids' well-being. How will they make it in life? How will you provide for them? What are the 101 things that could happen to them each day? The kids' health and safety can become a parental obsession.

These are real concerns, but you need not let them ruin your quality of life. At some point you must realize that anxiety is eroding your ability to function and enjoy life. Otherwise, you cannot sleep, and you suffer from insomnia. You easily become irritable over the smallest issue. You experience muscle tension. You develop chronic pains or symptoms for which no doctor can diagnose the cause. Your mind is not focused on what you need to accomplish, but rather you find yourself thinking too many thoughts at once, losing concentration and following the path of greatest worry.

I will not discuss the four or five types of clinically diagnosed anxiety disorders. For simplicity's sake, I will just give you the Chuck Pierce Anxiety Test. I have looked at many different books on anxiety, and then also looked back at my own experiences, to come up with these fifteen questions:

- Do you stay on the verge and tense when someone interrupts the order of your day or gets in the way of your latest deadline?
- Do you wake up tired and wonder how you will make it through the day without collapsing?

- Do you multitask out of necessity, but find yourself missing necessary steps in the process of getting your activities done?

- Are there times your mind seems frozen, and you cannot remember things like: Your name? The answer to a test question? Others' names? Your destination? What you went into another room to get? The question related to the phone call you just made?

- Does your body hurt? Do you have muscular tension? Headaches? Undiagnosed pain caused by this tension? Bowel problems? Fibromyalgia?

- Do you dread sleep as much as getting up? Is your sleep very restless? Do you wake up more than twice a night? Do you have night sweats? Nightmares? Sleep apnea?

- Do you have an abiding fear of being humiliated or judged as stupid, silly or awkward? Are you embarrassed in social circumstances or at times called crazy? Do you become tremulous as you anticipate speaking or performing in front of groups? Are you afraid that you will be accused falsely for the failure of something you are involved in?

- Will you do anything to avoid crowds, public appearances or speaking or performing in front of groups? Would you prefer to be alone?

- Are you obsessed with neatness and order? Or do you let a mess overwhelm you and add to your chaos?

- Do you immerse yourself in work, or do you have a difficult time finding work and staying focused and committed to your assignment?

- Are you afraid of a thunderstorm, a horse, a snake, a spider, being alone or being in closed places?

131

- When you think of the future, do you have a tingling, churning feeling inside?

- When someone mentions a scenario (which does not have to be about you) and a memory trigger occurs, do you find your heart palpitating, hands sweating, breath laboring and even numbness in your extremities?

- Do paying bills and taking care of other responsibilities overwhelm you?

- Do you find yourself compulsive about an issue such as your hair, your clothes, your food or something else?

Anxiety can become so intense that you obsessively make an attempt to get everything in order and keep everything in order. This is where simplicity is no longer the rule and complexity becomes the measure of your life. You become isolated and preoccupied with your fears. You anticipate the events that will trigger your anxiety. Your relationships suffer because of the excuses you make to avoid certain situations. Your life is filled with misunderstandings. You leave tension-producing scenarios quickly. You never wish to share with others or listen to others.

If this describes you and you had to answer yes to many of the questions on the Chuck Pierce Anxiety Test, then you need to realize a change is in order, as I did. You need a moment where you wake up and say, "Aha! This is not a normal way to live—I need to uncomplicate my life and emotions!" But you can only simplify your life if you face your anxiety issue, call it what it is (sin) and ask the Lord to help you deal with it. How I came to that moment of change and started to address my anxiety is the subject of the next chapter.

9

A Moment for Change

I want to share some steps that have led to my reformation and deliverance from anxiety, but first let me share one instance that awakened me to my need for change. Pam and I had been married for five years. I had graduated from college with honors and awards and had taken a job in Houston. During those years, we each had our own "normal" relationship with the Lord. We each had a prayer life, but our prayer lives were very private. We enjoyed the couple of churches we attended during that time, but we never got overly involved. We would teach Sunday school and attend special events, but we never really embraced the fellowship dynamic or sought closeness with others.

I immersed myself in work for a major energy company, and the blessings of the Lord were obviously on us, according to the world's view of success. You could say that through college and career, I had started a new life and had left behind the difficult story of my first eighteen years. And now, five years into our marriage, Pam and I were known as just a "good, solid couple."

But God! He chose to interrupt our lives. One night Pam and I were talking about sin and temptations, and I shared something that had occurred during the day at work. Pam said to me, "Chuck, ever since I have known you, you have always had a problem being decisive at crucial moments in your life. Unless you deal with this stronghold, we'll face some difficult times in the future!"

I was startled. God was bringing me to a point where I knew I had to choose. I must either deny my problem of double-mindedness—the result of fear and anxiety—or leave the past behind and choose to be healed. I was not sure what a "stronghold" was, but I decided I was willing to find out. I loved my wife more than anything, so I would do whatever was necessary to protect our covenant relationship. (I also knew that she was redheaded and still had a temper—the Maureen O'Hara type—and I really did not want to have a major brawl. Down deep, I knew she would win anyway.)

Therefore, I asked Pam, "What should I do?"

She said, "Get before the Lord and wait until He shows you the snare in your life and changes you. Don't sugarcoat your sin. Call your sin *sin*, and then ask the Holy Spirit to demolish it!"

This sounded simple, but I was not really sure how to proceed. I had never seen the relationship between fear, anxiety and sin. Still, I determined that sin would not have dominion in my life. This was the beginning of my change. I was setting myself up for a greater confrontation than I had known before. Not a confrontation with the person I loved the most on earth, my wife, but with the One who knows us best, the

Spirit of God! The Word of God says in Psalm 139:13 that God formed our inner parts and knit us together in our mothers' wombs. In my case, God was now ready to confront and transform what He had put together. The Spirit of the Lord was beginning to work out those fragmented places within me that had created fear and anxiety.

That night when I had my quiet time, I took the Word of God and read Romans 6 out loud to the Lord. I loved the Word, and I understood fairly well where things were in Scripture. Something unusual happened this time, though. I got to verse 14, "*Sin shall not have dominion over you,*" and I stopped. I looked up at the Lord and prayed differently than I had ever prayed before. I said, "Lord, is this true?"

As clearly as if someone were in the room with me, He said, *Yes!*

I then said, "Is this entire Book true?"

He then answered again and said, *Yes! Obey My Word!*

I found His voice penetrating. I found His Word alive. He did not say, *Believe,* but *Obey!* I knew I was starting a new journey.

He then began to penetrate me with His love. He took the chiseling power of His Word and began to go deep inside of me and break things away from my heart. He used His chisel to break old fears and to tear away insecurities that were covered by a coat of pride. He worked gently to uncover wounds that had not been healed. I could see areas that were scarred over and not healed properly. He was ready to further a restoration process in me that had stalled.

Four hours later, I came out of the room. Pam said that I looked like a different person. The next day, I would begin to act differently. We will discuss this further in a moment. First, let's take a look at someone from Scripture who had a similar problem with anxiety and also overcame it.

Martha or Mary?

One of the greatest personality studies in the Bible occurs in Luke 10, when we find Jesus visiting a home in Bethany. This home, Martha's house, seemed a refuge for Him from the crowds and the stress of His redemption task. We find that Jesus came to love this entire household: Martha, Mary and their brother, Lazarus. Luke 10:38–42 (AMP) tells this story:

> Now while they were on their way, it occurred that Jesus entered a certain village, and a woman named Martha received and welcomed Him into her house.
>
> And she had a sister named Mary, who seated herself at the Lord's feet and was listening to His teaching.
>
> But Martha [overly occupied and too busy] was distracted with much serving; and she came up to Him and said, Lord, is it nothing to You that my sister has left me to serve alone? Tell her then to help me [to lend a hand and do her part along with me]!
>
> But the Lord replied to her by saying, Martha, Martha, you are anxious and troubled about many things;
>
> There is need of only one or but a few things. Mary has chosen the good portion [that which is to her advantage], which shall not be taken away from her.

Martha is a good woman. However, she displays what is known as a *type A* personality. Such people are action oriented, but also emotional. They are constantly competing and are easily irritated by delays. Type A people have a low tolerance for frustration. They drive themselves and others very hard. Easily angered, they can be aggressive at times. The real problem comes because they live under a load of guilt if they relax or rest.

They usually know the answer to any question in a conversation and will even answer questions for you when you are asked. You cannot live without these people—but they are not easy to live with. People with this personality type accomplish a lot. They get things done! They are driven by a built-in need to accomplish things and to see the world around them change. However, they can become hasty in their work, and as Proverbs 21:5 (NLT) says, "Hasty shortcuts lead to poverty." Narrowly focused on the task at hand (or several tasks), type A people can miss the key riches of life.

Note that Martha opened the door of her house when Jesus arrived. Type A people are door openers. However, they want everyone in their household to operate the same way they operate. Martha became agitated with her sister because Mary chose to stop and listen to Jesus, the Messiah, as opposed to doing dishes and thereby missing the riches in what He had to say.

Evidently, while He was teaching, Martha interrupted and requested that He send Mary to the kitchen. Martha had lost focus on what the Lord was doing at the moment. The Word says she was distracted, and the word *distracted* means "dragging around in circles." She was caught in a loop of *doing* rather than *hearing*, and she wanted Mary to drag around in circles with her. That happens so many times with us. We become frustrated and irritable over the push to get a job done, and we want to place that emotional stress on everyone else and drag them through it, too.

Jesus addressed Martha by revealing her anxiety to her. He also addressed her troubled emotional state. He explained that Mary had chosen to capture the moment and gain lasting revelation that would propel her into the future and secure her appointed or dominion rest (a concept I cover more in a chapter still ahead).

Pam and I wrote a book called *One Thing! How to Keep Your Faith in a World of Chaos* (Destiny Image, 2006) that portrays the amazing ways we have broken through our crises by doing what the Lord tells us to do. Pam more naturally does the simple, one thing. I have learned to work at hearing and obeying. Once I hear, I must discipline myself to not complicate my faith, but just to act on heaven's orders. It is a process for me. Each of us is a "work in progress"!

Address Your Anxiety

Now, let me be the first to say that just because you address the problem of anxiety, that does not mean the problem is taken care of. However, by addressing the problem, getting the issue in the open and out of the hidden recesses of your emotions, you can then start the process of healing and becoming whole for your future. Your future certainly will be longer if you address this problem—hasty, anxious people use more adrenaline than others and eventually burn out more quickly.

During my four-hour meeting with the Lord, I started seeing my sin. I started calling my thoughts what they were—my own thoughts exalted above His—*sin*. Just as I gave you fifteen questions to answer on my anxiety test to see if you fall into the *Martha-Anxious* category, here are fifteen steps I have learned to take to break down anxiety. (Note that the first one is simply calling your sin for what it is, as I finally did.)

1. Be simple. Call your sin—*sin*.
2. Agree with the Word of God.
3. Allow the Word and the Spirit to work in you mightily to make you a child of God.
4. Forgive those who have hurt you in any way.
5. Break the power of isolation around you.

6. Become vulnerable.
7. Experience God's love.
8. Be willing to pray for others in order to see yourself healed.
9. Let go and lose control.
10. Give! Give! Give!
11. Submit quickly to His will even when you are confused by a circumstance.
12. Resist the enemy's voice that convinces you that you have failed. Rejoice evermore and align every situation of your life with God's perfect will.
13. Learn to listen to others so you can sense their emotional communication within their verbal communication.
14. Trust that God can send help and intervene in your life in time.
15. Be simple. Do what God tells you to do.

"We Do Not Share!"

After my meeting with the Lord and the chisel of His Word, change happened immediately. That was a Tuesday night. The next morning, I started my daily Bible reading as usual. The Spirit of God started working again. I was used to reading three chapters each day. I read one verse, and He said, *Don't go to the next verse until you believe and are willing to obey the one you just read.* The chapter was John 20, where the Lord sends His disciples to forgive. He showed me unforgiveness in my heart. He then instructed me to take a trip that weekend to East Texas to see my grandparents. Because of how painful our family situation was, they had chosen not to see their grandchildren again. Not only had I lost my dad, but I was disconnected from that whole side of the family.

However, it was Wednesday night, which was a "church" night. I had forsaken prayer meetings since college, but I got home from work and told Pam that I was tired of just going to church on Sunday morning and that I thought we should join the church I had felt a nudge toward a year prior. She smiled and said, "Let's go and see what they're about first."

We arrived to find out that they were having a Baptist business meeting. At the end of the meeting, I went forward with Pam in hand and said, "We're here to join the church."

The education director was leading the service. (They were without a pastor.) He looked at me in surprise and said, "We don't usually do that on Wednesday night."

I said, "Well, I'm here to say that I must do this tonight."

He looked a little perplexed, but said, "Let me get a card to take down your information."

On the way home from church, I told Pam about the trip to East Texas. She agreed to go with me. When we arrived at my grandparents' place, whom I had not seen in eleven years, they were shocked. I explained that even though so much hurt had happened in our family, I was very sorry that I had missed the last eleven years, and I asked if they would please forgive me for not coming sooner. They began to weep. The Lord began to heal.

I was moving forward. Reflecting on that time, Pam says the whole season became surreal because there was such a change in our lives. The next week, we attended church and Sunday school at our new church. We found that the young married couples were going on a retreat the next weekend, and Pam signed us up. On the retreat, something happened to move me forward even further—after it set me back a little. Thirty couples attended, and we each were asked to share about our lives, how we met, about our family and what we did. Our turn came, and I said firmly, "We are very private people, and we do not share!"

Oh my! I was fine moving forward with the Lord. However, now He had thrown in people. I tried to watch my every word because I really did not know how to share my past yet. Pam cringed at my statement and smiled graciously, and they moved on around the circle of couples.

At dinner, I chose a table where I hoped we could sit by ourselves. Two couples came over and sat with us anyway. One of the guys just hooted over my statement. Little did he know that I meant my reply. He could not believe I wanted to be so private. He did not have a private bone in his body. God used him to break down the ice wall I had built against relationships and the fear I had of sharing anything about my past. We three couples became close friends and prayer partners, which started the next stage of healing for me.

"I Loved Your Dad"

Every Friday night we three couples would get together and paint. All of us were creative. I had not painted since the tragedy of my family breakup. Pam knew I could paint, though, because she knew about some contests I had won. The six of us painted, prayed and worshiped. Before long, I was no longer private. I had shared the major hurts of my family, and I found out that each person among the six had his or her own story. Isolation had broken. We had moved past work and business relationships into having true spiritual fellowship.

I looked forward to each weekend. Those Fridays became my Sabbaths. Each one became a time of healing. I was getting delivered from being anxious, performance-minded and a workaholic, all of which I had used to cover over the real issues in my life. My health also began to shift for the better, whereas before, I had suffered with many chronic issues: severe allergies, heart and blood pressure issues and, mainly, overwhelming migraines.

I felt the Spirit of God directing me on a daily basis. One day, I was driving to work and suddenly God's presence filled the car. He began to pour His love out on me. The love was so overpowering that I could not drive. I pulled to the side of the road in a busy Houston suburb and said, "Lord, Your love is so overwhelming. What have I done to deserve this love?"

He answered immediately, *This was how much I loved your dad.*

I was shocked. I knew what we had lived through. He then said, *Receive what he never experienced.* I saw God's love. I saw how He loves us no matter what. His love is pure and clean. I saw and experienced a depth of His love that day that changed me.

This accelerated our life in the Spirit. Our path shifted. Pam and I call those years "The Glory Years." We experienced so much of God's restoration power. So much healing occurred in our souls. I was changed from Anxious Martha to Seeking Mary. However, notice that it was a process. Was I ever anxious again? Absolutely. Escaping into freedom was and is an ongoing process for me, as you will read in the next chapter. However, I had begun progressing greatly "in Him," and a process had begun that could never be stopped.

You Are a Work in Progress

The repeated attention we give to any one thing shapes us tremendously. I was now giving my best attention to the Lord, as Mary had done. When you do that, the stimuli of the world lets go, and you begin to transform your thinking. (We will

142

talk more about that in the next chapter, too.) Here is what happens:

1. You develop *new* thought patterns.
2. Your memories of wounding and defeat stop overpowering your *hope* for the future.
3. You start moving by *faith* and not just by emotional feeling.
4. You destroy secret fantasies and enter into a *new reality*.
5. You are willing to enter *Father's Course of Discipline* because discipline will define your gift.
6. You are not afraid to try *new* things and develop *new* skills.
7. You recognize pain and defeat its power, and you experience a *new release of joy*.
8. You *cast out fear*. No longer are you afraid of the night, but you listen to your dream life.
9. You allow the Lord to have *access* to your heart. You do not fear circumcision, for the momentary pain is rolling away past reproaches.
10. You can detect and break (soul) ties with *past seasons*, and you can *mourn* and *move on*.

Move into the New

Get on a progressive upward walk with the Lord. You can make this shift. In the next chapter, we will discuss much more about "the cares of this world" and the stress they create. However, I want you to know that you can escape into peace. This is your moment for change.

A new day waits for those whom anxiety has held captive. Instead of choosing fright and flight, choose standing, resisting and overcoming. Be vulnerable and expose yourself (slowly) to the triggers that have haunted you. Instead of developing catastrophic survival skills, develop peace skills. Learn to wait, be patient and choose the best way.

I am a work in progress, and I can tell you from experience that the Lord can create peace that passes understanding where anxiety once reigned.

10

Stress Can Work for You

After reading the last couple of chapters, I think you can get a feel for why I became the anxious type. We all go through severe trials. This is the fodder for our faith. The problem comes when we allow the stress of trials to overtake us. Also, we can find ourselves overwhelmed when we do not co-labor through the hard moments of our lives with the Holy Spirit. By bearing our burdens in our own flesh, we allow the stress of those burdens to have an adverse effect on our organs. (I will discuss this more later in the chapter.) Then there is this incredible scenario that Paul talks about in Romans 7:15: "I don't really understand myself, for I want to do what is right, but I don't do it. Instead, I do what I hate" (NLT). In other words, the things I hate the most, things I see as detrimental to my life, I begin to experience and end up doing myself. Breaking the cycle of sin, carnality, hurt, grief and even self-righteousness is not always the easiest thing to accomplish.

We must not forget that through the Spirit there is a *way of escape*! First Corinthians 10:13 says, "No temptation has overtaken you except such as is common to man; but God is faithful, who will not allow you to be tempted beyond what you are able, but with the temptation will also make the way of escape, that you may be able to bear it." How do we escape from a trauma-filled past and restore the childlike faith we lost along the way? I believe this is the key question someone who plans on leaving a life of anxiety and crossing over into a life of faith must ask.

We have already discussed Martha's anxiety problem. However, Martha was not the only one in the Bible to go through a trial, make mistakes and be corrected. All of the people you find recorded in the "Faith Chapter," Hebrews 11, lived in difficult times, experienced stressful circumstances and resisted being taken over by anxiety. Sarah and Abraham were impatient in developing their future. Elisha's servant, Gehazi, had an anxiety problem seemingly linked with money. Jeremiah seemed to have a terrible anxiety issue and had to be confronted by the Lord on more than one occasion in an attempt to adjust his emotions. I could go on and on with character analyses of key biblical examples, but note that these and many others found their way of escape, exercised their faith and entered a peace and rest that passed all understanding.

Jesus Was Different

Jesus taught and demonstrated what His Father wanted to be expressed in the earth. He said,

> Your eye is a lamp that provides light for your body. When your eye is good, your whole body is filled with light. But

when your eye is bad, your whole body is filled with darkness. And if the light you think you have is actually darkness, how deep that darkness is!

No one can serve two masters. For you will hate one and love the other; you will be devoted to one and despise the other. You cannot serve both God and money [mammon in the KJV].

That is why I tell you not to worry about everyday life— whether you have enough food and drink, or enough clothes to wear. Isn't life more than food, and your body more than clothing? Look at the birds. They don't plant or harvest or store food in barns, for your heavenly Father feeds them. And aren't you far more valuable to him than they are? Can all your worries add a single moment to your life?

And why worry about your clothing? Look at the lilies of the field and how they grow. They don't work or make their clothing, yet Solomon in all his glory was not dressed as beautifully as they are. And if God cares so wonderfully for wildflowers that are here today and thrown into the fire tomorrow, he will certainly care for you. Why do you have so little faith?

So don't worry about these things, saying, "What will we eat? What will we drink? What will we wear?" These things dominate the thoughts of unbelievers, but your heavenly Father already knows all your needs. Seek the Kingdom of God above all else, and live righteously, and he will give you everything you need.

So don't worry about tomorrow, for tomorrow will bring its own worries. Today's trouble is enough for today.

Matthew 6:22–34, NLT

Throughout the last thirty-plus years of my life, I have memorized these Scripture verses, quoted the words in many hard situations and walked in their revelation and power on many occasions, but at times I still have to remind myself what the Lord said to us here. This passage develops the relationship between conscience, devotion and our emotions. ❦ To keep my conscience pure, I have learned that my *way of escape* has been through praise, thanksgiving, prayer and intercessions.

The purity of our conscience is linked with whom we serve. How we serve plays a role in the development of our emotional well-being. For example, our devotion to self-preservation can create much worry in our lives. Our connection to the culture in a materialistic society can create a tremendous emotional upheaval in our lives—especially when we know that we ought to be connected to the Kingdom culture we were transferred into by the Lord's sacrifice on Calvary. Simply put, if you are devoted to money and are striving for success in the eyes of a world system, you will find yourself entangled by cares of the world and overwhelmed with anxiety.

Jesus came and walked through much conflict, but it did not entangle Him. He maintained complete emotional stability and balance before the Father. *He proved to us that we could alleviate anxiety.*

How Do You Respond to Each Day?

"So don't worry about tomorrow; tomorrow will bring its own worries." Because Jesus said we are to live this way, and He could only say what the Father was saying, I know this is a true statement. But how do we "do" this statement? How do we live it?

❦ Each day, we must make many choices. Choice is an act of our wills. The will is dependent upon the interaction of the spirit of man with the Spirit of God. We are to align the way we think with the way God thinks in a situation. To determine our success at doing this, we need to ask ourselves, *Do I live with simple, childlike faith, or do I approach each event in my life with a complicated, complex view of the situation?*

Biblically, time is a cycle linked with our bodily, soulish and spiritual responses. How we process the events of time in our lives creates what I call "The Syndrome of Life." The stress of each event molds our responses to life. God made us in such a way that the events in our lives condition us. External stress creates internal development. Over time, how we process the stressors of life influences who we are and molds the way people perceive us and the way we perceive the world around us.

The body has a stress response. This response provides the energy to adapt to a changing environment. Because the changing world around us continues to bombard us, we find ourselves caught in a dichotomy between moving from faith to faith or stress to stress. We are a people programmed to survive. Survival is built into the makeup of our DNA structure. When we overcome one of life's tests, our survival instinct grows stronger. When one of life's tests overcomes us, a breakdown and a wounding weaken our system. The goal to survive is still within us, but our ability is weakened. So remember to take one day at a time and overcome rather than being overcome!

Fright or Flight?

We are all familiar with the human body's response to a perceived threat or danger. In high school biology, we learned about the fight-or-flight response that releases hormones such as adrenaline and cortisol into our systems, giving us that burst of energy required to run away from or physically resist danger. This response is also often referred to as the "fight, fright, or flight response." That label more appropriately

149

describes my own experience! The following statement from Victor Pease's book *Anxiety into Energy* really spoke to me: "Stress response creates the energy to fight, to run away from danger, to work and play."[1] The problem is that if we do not learn to embrace the stress of the day, the way the Lord taught us, we fall into fear, run from our responsibilities or fight unnecessary battles.

Two types of behaviors are important to our stress responses. They are voluntary and involuntary. The voluntary nervous system is linked with the will. When we desire to do something, we must consciously make a decision about it. All through the day, we find ourselves making decisions. When I was growing up, my mother taught me to get up each day and make a list. The objective was to complete what was on the list before the day was out or by a certain appointed time each day. I had voluntarily surrendered to my mother's order for each day. I had a goal. However, when you live in a life situation where you are frequently interrupted by violence, arguing and trauma, as I was, accomplishing your list becomes difficult. Not only do you become frustrated, but eventually you become defeated. Eventually there is no real order to your day, and your mind and emotions become stressed by each thought about the things you need to accomplish.

On top of this, you live with the anxiety of wondering what kind of adverse situation will enter your day and re-order everything around you. Your voluntary system wishes to speak, but fear overwhelms the process. For example, you might need to remember an important fact, but you do not have time to collect your thoughts.

All the while, the involuntary, or autonomic, nervous system is working overtime in an attempt to keep up with all the stimuli you are trying to process. The autonomic system controls such physiological functions as breathing, heart rate, hormone secretion and the smooth muscle contractions of the intestines. With all this going on inside you, you can easily understand why an inability to properly handle stress can so negatively affect your health.

How we perceive an event produces the basis of all of our communication. Perception is how we use our senses—taste, sight, touch, smell and hearing. Perception of an event in time is usually thought of as a conscious decision on our part, which we based on the facts presented. However, unconscious elements from our emotions are also factored into our perceptions. Anger, disappointment and fear create a tension that accumulates within the spirit, soul and body. This tension can stem from residual past experiences where embedded stressors within us have remained dormant. Some of these dormant stimuli escape us and may go unnoticed until pressure is applied. They are not always obvious in us or to us, but over time, they have weakened our ability to cope.

Stress Is Like an Onion

We might have to be peeled like an onion to get to the very core of the strength and destiny that God created us to display. An onion is not a vegetable we usually eat by itself. The main purpose of an onion is to add flavor to the meal prepared and set before us. Stressors from life's situations are like an onion. If we process stressors correctly, they can create great flavor in the overall "stew of life."

Think about peeling an onion. You must grasp it firmly with the hand you use the least, then take a sharp knife and slice the onion with the opposite hand. One way that we process a stressful situation is to take firm hold of it. We must think differently. Usually we have an orderly way of dealing with most things in our life. However, when an unexpected, stressful situation occurs, we must rely upon skills that we perhaps do not normally use. There is a creative power in us that is not accessed unless we are forced to go beyond our current knowledge. On many occasions, we never tap into the creative power of the side of the brain that we use less often unless we go through a narrow place of stress. That narrow place presses out the best of the creativity hidden deep within us.

During the process of peeling an onion, the fumes can overwhelm you and create a river of tears. This happens if you expose too much of the onion at one time. Emotionally, we must be careful not to expose the raw nerve endings of our being when we process a stressful situation. We must watch carefully, remain as silent as possible, pray and wait for revelation on how to walk forward. Some would say being "cool, calm and collected" is key. Overreacting can lead to many unnecessary tears in the process.

Peeling off the onion skin proceeds until the best part of an onion is exposed. When the outer layer is peeled away, the onion is ready to use. All the while, the objective is not to lose too much of the onion and not to allow the process to overwhelm you with weeping. Many times, a stressful situation peels away layer after layer of our emotional being. But we must remember that the Spirit of the Lord can use this peeling process to expose the best part of our core—that part in us that can be used to flavor and touch many lives.

I like what Jesus said when Peter was stressed out over the prophecy about Jesus' death. Jesus told him that Satan desired to sift him. Then Jesus added that He would pray, and that when Peter had made it through, he would help many others (see Luke 22:31–32). During every stressful situation, the enemy of our souls longs to take advantage of us.

Can stress work for you to flavor your life and the lives of others? Or will you become emotionally overwhelmed by it, let weeping overtake you in the process and therefore miss the taste of perception in that moment? Will you allow all the stressors in your life to expose the core of your being? Will your stressors sweeten your soul so that many others will fully see the best in your personality coming forth?

During every pressured circumstance of our lives, we should allow the peeling process of the Spirit of God to work. Flavor and favor will arise in our lives. When we allow stress to work properly in our lives, many others will benefit.

Stress—a Blessing or a Curse?

A blessing is made up of good words that confer mercy, grace, favor, praise, happiness, adoration and benefits to others. A curse contains bad words uttered to produce harm. Like good or bad words, stress can be a blessing or a curse. Not all stress is bad. Stress is not meant to be damaging for everybody. We should thrive in a stressful situation and use that moment to build our confidence and strength in the Lord.

Look what Isaiah 40:27–31 (AMP) says:

> Why, O Jacob, do you say, and declare, O Israel, My way and my lot are hidden from the Lord, and my right is passed over without regard from my God?
>
> Have you not known? Have you not heard? The everlasting God, the Lord, the Creator of the ends of the earth, does not faint or grow weary; there is no searching of His understanding.
>
> He gives power to the faint and weary, and to him who has no might He increases strength [causing it to multiply and making it to abound].

> Even youths shall faint and be weary, and [selected] young men shall feebly stumble and fall exhausted;
> But those who wait for the Lord [who expect, look for, and hope in Him] shall change and renew their strength and power; they shall lift their wings and mount up [close to God] as eagles [mount up to the sun]; they shall run and not be weary, they shall walk and not faint or become tired.

If we handle stress properly, it can fire us up and motivate us to complete our projects and overcome obstacles in our way. We will find ourselves receiving favor because we are overcome with praise in the midst of our trials. David proclaimed,

> In my distress [when seemingly closed in] I called upon the Lord and cried to my God; He heard my voice out of His temple (heavenly dwelling place), and my cry came before Him, into His [very] ears. . . .
> For You cause my lamp to be lighted and to shine; the Lord my God illumines my darkness.
> For by You I can run through a troop, and by my God I can leap over a wall.
>
> Psalm 18:6, 28–29, AMP

When we encounter a challenge, we must rise up to meet it. The rising-up portion is a small moment of time. The thrill of overcoming becomes a testimony that endures. Think about David's approach when he faced Goliath. He remembered the stress of facing the lion and the bear. He had overcome both. The stress of his moments of testing had become a testimony. In his present circumstance facing the giant, he relied on the memory of those past stressors to encourage himself in his present stress. He then received strength for the present challenge. He overcame in this situation as well as the former two. The stress of the giant situation was a curse for Israel, but became a blessing for David. His victory over it would set the course for his future.

Dr. Archibald D. Hart, in *The Hidden Link Between Adrenaline and Stress*, writes,

> The word stress means different things to different people. It is a multifaceted response that includes changes in perception, emotions, behavior and physical functioning. Some think of it only as tension, others as anxiety. Some think of it as good, others as bad. The truth is that we all need a certain amount of stress to keep us alive, although too much of it becomes harmful to us. . . . When most of us use the term, stress, we usually are referring to this harmful aspect—overstress. This "ebb and flow" effect is crucial to keep in mind if we never allow a calming after the storm, the storm becomes a hurricane. . . . It is these more subtle threats that produce the greatest amount of stress damage. Things that worry us, prod us, scare or frighten us—when there is nothing we can do about them—can be the most destructive of all. Perhaps this is why Jesus (who had many good things to say about controlling stress) told us, "Let not your heart be troubled, neither let it be afraid" (John 14:27).[2]

We all experience stress. Life is movement. For forward movement, one must face stress. To move forward in our lives, we must process stressors properly. That way, stress can turn into energy. How you apply pressure to an object creates movement and momentum. Stress can be very good if we manage the pressures around us. If we manage stress well, we tend to accelerate into our destined role in life. However, if stress manages us, we are filled with tension and anxiety. We must divert the negative side of stress and receive the power that advances us forward to solve the problems of each day.

How do you handle stress? Are you seemingly "in control" or "out of control" in the situations you face? How you perceive yourself and react in a given decision-making situation determines your stress level. Your perception of the situation and of who you are, as well as your level of authority, determines your energy level. Self-confidence and staying in control produce energy. This leads to accomplishment, self-satisfaction and forward movement into the role for which God destined you.

The Stress of Making Decisions

Major life changes such as divorce, the death of a spouse or losing a job certainly generate stress. Oh, but then there are the little foxes! The *greater* sources of stress for most of us are not the big things that enter our lives. What really stresses us are those life issues that seem minor, but then at the end of the day, overtake us. We usually have grace for the "big issues," but the "little issues" add up, and we eventually break under the weight of all the burdens we have accumulated throughout a season. The little things happen on a daily basis. When enough of them accumulate, getting up and ready for the workday ahead can then be overwhelming. What to wear? Whom to meet? The day-to-day hassles of decision making can literally push us over an edge, out of calmness and into the realm of overreaction.

Our world is filled with stressors. We experience stress because of our friends, family, work, city, transportation in the city, bad drivers, weather and on and on. God designed us to walk in stress! He also created us with the ability to make right decisions when a stressor enters and offers us an opportunity to rise to the occasion or bow out in defeat. In the Garden, He gave Adam complete liberty to decide the names of the animals and to oversee the cultivation process. He also released Adam and Eve creatively to multiply. He then set a boundary and required them not to cross that one boundary. If they would obey, they would prosper. They were called to watch over what humankind had been given and decide daily on how to further the blessings in their environment. If they needed wisdom, they could commune with the One who placed them in the Garden. If they needed creative insights, through their dialogue with the Creator they could find new ways of accomplishing each day's activities.

If Adam and Eve disobeyed, however, they would experience undue pressure and warfare. Therefore, some outside force had to sway their decision-making ability. The enemy knew that he had to break down the first man and woman's defense system. This "breakdown" would cause a decay in the ultimate best that they were created to experience. Instead of moving toward the process of fullness of joy, wrong decisions would create hurt, loss and the inability to freely take dominion and occupy the space in time they had been given.

Like Adam and Eve before us, many times we make wrong decisions. And also like them, each breakdown of our defenses causes a decay in our movement into the ultimate best God has for us. Wrong decisions still create a different process of life and movement from the one God originally intended for us to experience.

In my book *Redeeming the Time: Get Your Life Back on Track with the God of Second Opportunities* (Charisma House, 2009), I fully explain the process we must go through to regain our authority. Every generation must learn the process of choice in the midst of trials, stressors and anxious times. Joshua had the dubious task of leading a people forth who had made wrong choices forty years prior. I believe this is why we find Joshua admonishing the people to "choose for yourselves this day whom you will serve" (Joshua 24:15).

157

Choices can be overwhelming. If we tend to lean on our own understanding, we can make the wrong choice. In Proverbs 16:25 we find these words: "There is a way that seems right to a man, but its end is the way of death." In contrast, the words in Proverbs 3:5–6 have become some of my life Scriptures: "Trust in the LORD with all your heart, and lean not on your own understanding; in all your ways acknowledge Him, and He shall direct your paths." God can set our course and our mode of action in any situation. That is why stress can be a blessing, not a curse. When we process stress properly, it can work for us by motivating us to take action along the path of God's call for us. When we follow His course of action and not our own, our direct, intimate contact with Him will propel us into life's best.

Usually the root of all your fear and anxiety is embedded in a situation that created mistrust in your life. Mistrust wars against trust. Mistrust is determined to get you into a place of self-reliance so you miss God's course of action for you that will overcome anxiety in every situation. God is capable of straightening out your path. Relying on Him and waiting for Him to intervene with wisdom is not easy. However, remember that when we wait, He is straightening our path. And His path for us will be much simpler than any path we could discover on our own!

11

Faith: The Right Framework

In his book *Why We Make Mistakes*, Joseph Hallinan says, "A great many day-to-day errors come about because we frame, or look at, an issue in a wrong way."[1] *How* we frame an issue can greatly affect our response to it. No matter what the issue, faith creates the right framework! In Hebrews 11:3 we find, "By faith we understand that the worlds [during the successive ages] were framed (fashioned, put in order, and equipped for their intended purpose) by the word of God, so that what we see was not made out of things which are visible" (AMP).

Pam talked about faith, focus and function in the first chapter. When God created the world, He spoke. His voice created the framework for all things. For us to have the right perception of something, we must see how He framed the situation we find confronting us. When we do not see the right frame around a situation, that means we have not allowed faith to develop properly. I find the antidote for anxiety is faith. When we wait for faith to develop, we mount up with wings of eagles. Eagles have keen eyesight. If we mount up with faith, we see God's frame—and then we have the right perspective in any situation.

Our carnal minds war to hold us captive to anxious thoughts, and our perspective can overwhelm God's perspective. This is another way of saying that most of our errors in decision making come because we do not develop God's way of thinking in our lives. We can allow sorrow and grief to keep us from seeing God's way for us to overcome. By not pressing past hard circumstances, we can lose vision and eventually choose to go backward in the hope of finding "the good old days" we once experienced. We can actually put a death curse on our future by refusing to see God's ways through our desert and past the giants we face. The people of God in the wilderness slandered the promise they had been given because the giants overwhelmed their perspective and became bigger in their sight than the God who had ordained them to receive great blessings.

Carnality can take a different form and manifest in addictions, rejection and obsessive behaviors. A strong compulsion to be "doing something" can overwhelm us. There were times that taking a vacation produced more stress in me than constantly working. If we took a long weekend, I spent the first two days thinking of everything that could go wrong while we were away. Then on the third day, I would enjoy about an hour of relaxation before I started making a list of the things I needed to do when I returned. Then there were constant thoughts of what I might have left undone.

My inability to concentrate for long on a relaxing activity created more stress for me than trying to relax was worth. I did not have an anger problem, but I did get aggravated easily. Life could become exhausting quickly. I was never a particularly depressed type, but I could feel a noticeable letdown after the weekends because I had to redirect my drive. Then there were the headaches, which I will come back to shortly.

These are all forms of carnality. I loved the Lord. I sought the Lord. However, I did not really allow the Lord to *be* the Lord. This gave the enemy unnecessary and legitimate access to my soulish nature.

The Enemy Does Not Play Fair

In dangerous times, the enemy works overtime to discourage us and produce internal friction in our souls. He attempts to get us to hold on to old ways of thinking that lead to an ignorance of present truth. He longs to find a way to get us to participate with him. You and I must remove the hidden effects of trauma in us so that the enemy cannot use our hurts to convince us that God is not good or that He is holding out on us in some way. This is what the enemy did with the first man and woman in the Garden.

✱✱The enemy not only wants to *occupy* our souls and minds, but he wants to *vex* our spirits! He must find ways to disconnect us from communion with God. This dulls our intuition and robs us of an overcoming testimony. He annoys, agitates and confounds us, and he strives to make us anxious over our destiny. The enemy employs schemes and tactics to change times and laws to make our faith empty. He understands the power of unity better than we do, and he knows how to thwart the power of oneness with our Creator. Much anxiety comes because we agree to go along with the enemy's covenant-breaking strategies.

The enemy's goal is to make us fail to counteract faith destroyers. He wants to keep us from escaping slavery and plundering him! He creates *apathy and passivity*, making us dull, unfeeling, barren or inactive. He tempts us to be lazy or fall into *indolence*, and then he controls us with poverty. He longs to develop in us a mind of exaltation that leads us into being conceited and complacent. Our pride then makes us think we know it all (see Job 32:13). His ultimate goal is to block heaven, block our spirits and block our creative thinking. I call this having no *illumination* (see Job 9:11; Psalm 136:4). We then become anxious, and our thoughts reflect our anxiety.

The War to Transform Our Minds

Remember the scarecrow in *The Wizard of Oz*? His heart cry was, *"If I only had a brain!"* You and I have a brain. How we use this organ is the key to our success from season to season. I am trusting the Lord to reform and transform our thoughts so we end this season strong and begin the next season stronger. To accomplish this, we must think differently. Recently, the Lord spoke to me and said, *Begin to pray that My people change their brains to think like Me.*

The human brain is unique and complex, giving us the power to think, plan, speak, imagine and create. This amazing organ controls body temperature, blood pressure, breathing and heart rate. While God aligns our hearts' desires with His beating heart, the brain controls the physical beating of our hearts. It also coordinates our physical motion when walking, talking, standing or sitting. As we do all these things, the brain takes in the incredible flood of information acquired from our senses. We need to be aware of how our brains are functioning. How we perceive what we see, hear, smell, taste and touch will affect our discernment this year. Therefore, our brains need to stay active, healed and properly functioning for us to be transformed into new, sharp threshing instruments for God.

The brain also allows us to process emotional stimuli. The brain lets us reason, emote and dream. The brain, spinal cord and peripheral nerves make up our complex, integrated information-processing and control system. How you and I "let go" and allow the Spirit of God to realign our control centers this year will be a key to our success in the days ahead.

Repentance is the process of "changing our brains" so we think the way the Lord thinks. When we repent, we turn and walk away from a path that prevents us from seeing the desires of God manifest in our lives. When we turn and think the way God would have us think, we turn onto a path that brings life, and life abundant. So keep turning until you have turned into the new path ahead.

This all seems so complex in a book on simplicity. But without the mind being stayed on the Lord, we have only a slight chance—if any—for peace in our lives. In Isaiah 26:3, God says He will keep in perfect peace those whose minds are stayed on Him. Can peace be a simple experience for us? Let's look at that further. In these days, we must remember that the enemy will try to wear down our minds. Look what Daniel says in Daniel 7:

> As I looked, this horn made war with the saints and prevailed over them. . . .
> And he shall speak words against the Most High [God] and shall wear out the saints of the Most High and think to change the time [of sacred feasts and holy days] and the law; and the saints shall be given into his hand for a time, two times, and half a time [three and one-half years].
>
> Verses 21, 25, AMP

163

Do not let the enemy wear you down. Daniel also says,

> Until the Ancient of Days came, and judgment was given to the saints of the Most High [God], and the time came when the saints possessed the kingdom. . . .
>
> But the judgment shall be set [by the court of the Most High], and they shall take away his dominion to consume it [gradually] and to destroy it [suddenly] in the end.
>
> And the kingdom and the dominion and the greatness of the kingdom under the whole heavens shall be given to the people of the saints of the Most High; His kingdom is an everlasting kingdom, and all the dominions shall serve and obey Him.
>
> Verses 22, 26–27, AMP

Do not grow weary! There comes a moment in time when we overcome in our crisis. There comes a time when we recognize the enemy's plan and his tactics and outwit him. There comes a time when we break through, and the power of the enemy's control breaks. This was the case with Daniel. He brought heaven into the earth realm through intercession and gained revelation for generations to come. You and I can also triumph in the midst of changes.

The mind, heart, emotions and well-being of the soul are intricately connected. Usually, the enemy's goal in persecution is not to see us burned at the stake. To *persecute* actually means to wear down the mind and remove the strength. This disables a person from having the rightly connected thought process for success and prosperity in days of turmoil. One of the ways the enemy wears us down, then, is by causing the complexities of life to overcome our thoughts and emotions.

If the enemy can bombard us with thoughts that produce fear and anxiety, he can then remove our ability to manifest the will of God in our lives. The pure in heart see God (see Matthew 5:8). If our minds are weary, our hearts ache and we lose vision for our present and our future. Do not allow the enemy to cause you to lose focus on your inheritance. Your inheritance is your portion. This is your vineyard! The enemy is contending with us over how "the earth is the LORD's, and the fulness thereof" (Psalm 24:1, KJV).

I believe the Body of Christ must evaluate every resource available and think in a different way. The adult brain encodes knowledge and skills, joys and regrets, plans for the future. It makes us aware of ourselves by producing thoughts linked with our hearts' desires and our belief system. The brain reflects our emotions by producing thoughts that will cause self-preservation after we have been hurt. The brain is constantly changing the landscape of how we see the world. Our mental landscape now is very different than it was ten years ago. The brain is constantly updating itself. We would be wise to follow its lead and adapt a more analytical and creative approach. Our mindset must change as the times around us change.

God never changes, however. He is stable and creative in all things. We can see Him and know Him. We can see ourselves and the world around us through His perspective.

Use "It" or Lose "It"

The brain is there to keep us alive. Brain cells carry messages to our bodies and cognitively connect thought patterns that cause us to be creative and efficient in all of our assignments. When we quit using a portion of our brain, we lose the functioning power of those cells.

The brain is a wonderful weapon—if we learn to use it effectively. The brain has memory, math, language and spatial

165

zones. Some of us use portions of it with great ease and leave other portions to lie dormant. Some of us have emotional blocks linked with our emotions that keep portions of our brains from being active. If our emotions are not healthy, our brains will not develop properly. For instance, you can form a blockade or fear about learning something. You can form a fear about water and never learn to swim. You can convince yourself that you do not like math and that it is not necessary for your life, so consequently you never develop your math capabilities. This cripples you throughout life. In the case of math skills, for example, it might negate the sequencing order skills necessary for you to succeed in certain situations.

I remember Pam once saying to me, "The only course that I have ever had trouble with was algebra."

Of course, Pam has excelled in any language, history or English literature class she has ever taken. People who read our book *One Thing* always say, "I know when Pam is writing and when you are writing. Your styles and simplicity of expression are so different." Most see that Pam expresses herself well in written forms of communication.

When we were in college, I told Pam, "Pretend that math is language, and use your strong language abilities to process the math problems." She tried it and actually earned a B in all her advanced math courses. This broke down her fear of learning in the subject she feared most. If she had done the opposite and given up on math entirely, she would not have progressed the way she did. When we do not use a portion of our brain, we lose its functioning power.

The Heart Thinks

Of course, more is involved in our life processes than the brain. Our blood circulates throughout the body, supplying life-giving nutrients to each part. The circulatory or cardio-vascular system provides blood to the organs of the body from cell to cell, which helps stabilize our body temperature. The heart, lungs and blood vessels, which include arteries, veins and capillaries, all work together with about five liters of blood (in the average adult body) to create this circle of life flow.

This blood within us does more than just supply physical life. Leviticus 17:11 says, "For the life of the flesh is in the blood . . . it is the blood that makes atonement for the soul." We can already see that blood takes on a spiritual significance for our very souls. But there is still more. Proverbs 23:7 says, "For as he thinks in his heart, so is he." Without taking this verse out of context, we can see that the heart is associated with—if not the controller of—our thought processes. Obviously the brain is where our knowledge is stored. And yet this verse indicates that it is not the brain thinking, but the heart! If the heart is thinking, that means it is involving both our developed belief system as well as information that we have accumulated and categorized in our brain. And if that is the case, then our cardiovascular system—which cycles blood to and from the heart—is responsible for the transportation of our thoughts. So when the heart is pumping blood, it is carrying a thought system throughout the entire body. In essence, all of our organs are responding to the way our hearts think.

Therefore, if we are anxious and are not thinking correctly, this flows through our entire body. But when we hear and agree with God, the power of our communion flows through the spirit, soul and body, sanctifying us and enabling us to move forward into life with the confidence of God. The stress of life does not wear us down, because when two are in agreement, we find Him in our midst. When we are one with Him,

167

life does become simple. We overcome. Greater is He who is in us, than He who is in the world (see 1 John 4:4).

We are meant to and made to overcome the curse of stress and have all stress work for our good.

Blow a Trumpet—Sound an Alarm!

Stress begins in the mind but ends in the body. This is important to remember. There is no such thing as stress only being in the mind. Our bodies are designed to protect us from stress. Dr. Archibald Hart states that the body's protective system has three components:

1. An *alarm system* designed to sound a warning when something goes wrong. Pain is a part of this system. It tells us when body tissue is being damaged.
2. An *activating system* designed to prepare us for action in response to the alarm. This is an emergency system triggered and sustained by adrenaline arousal. It prepares us for the "fight or flight" response.
3. A *recovery system* designed to provide healing, recuperation, and revitalization. It is the neglect of this recovery system that leads to premature heart disease and many of the other painful consequences of stress.[2]

Have you ever had a "red flag in the Spirit" waved in your face? Every time the Lord alarms His people, He triggers stress in us. This mobilizes our bodies' defenses against the approaching hostile, threatening, challenging or dangerous events in our environment. Many times these are warnings to counteract the events that are approaching. How we mobilize during these events will be reflective of the way we manage, or process, the resulting stress.

"Blow the trumpet in Zion! And sound an alarm in My holy mountain! . . . For the day of the LORD is coming," Joel 2:1 says. There is a certain sound that initiates movement and awareness. In Bible times, the trumpet would sound to let the people know when it was time to assemble for war.

I think sometimes that we stay in a place of anxiety over impending attacks, rather than just waiting for the sound to advance. Yet the *alarm system* in us can be activated properly. When we hear the alarm, we can react properly, and as a result realize victory at the end of a situation. However, if we are anxiously walking in the fear of the future and all that the stressors in the world around us can bring, we can damage our being. We become like the boy who cried wolf—when the "wolf" actually comes inside our boundaries, we have no strength to react properly.

If we anticipate war long enough, our system stays in a state of alarm, or on high alert, as I talked about earlier. And when the time comes to activate and move forward, we then find that we have already spent much of our energy in anxiously waiting. If we heed our warnings or alarms, though, and activate our faith, we will always walk in restoration and recovery.

Changes Make Us Stress-Prone

Not only do many of us live life in the fast lane, where we have little time for real rest, but the social and moral values at large around us are changing rapidly. Trying to remain in harmony with God's absolute standards and keeping our conscience clear can become more and more stressful. My children often remind me how much pressure they get from peers to "go with the crowd" and throw away their Christian values. However, Pam and I have attempted to make them understand and recognize how uniquely they have been created, each having a unique purpose and personality.

I am a mobilizer. That is part of my unique personality that God can use for His purposes. I love to connect with people and encourage them to connect with others. In a mobile society, you are either overwhelmed by the bigness of everything or you learn to make the world small. I travel approximately two hundred and fifty thousand miles a year. I can be "at home" in China or Vermont. My call is to the nations of the earth. The mobile society we live in works for me.

For a season, Pam followed me as I ventured out to find my place in the world. However, cool, calm, collected Pam now loves her home in Denton. I pack and repack, sometimes three times a week. When I ask her to go along with me, she sees the process as a little overwhelming. She helps me pack, but she prefers to tend the home, her church and my family (who live close to us). She gets involved in city activities, attends Master Gardener continuing education courses and stays very involved with our children and grandchildren.

When she was a child, Pam moved constantly. Each move became a major upheaval that required living in a new home, changing schools, adjusting to new friends, locating a church home and learning a new culture. There came a time in our marriage when she wanted to settle down, begin to raise our family and establish roots. Because she experienced so many life changes as a child and young adult, the stress of constant life changes now could work against her joy. I believe Pam knows what true joy is, and she knows how to experience the best God has for her life by resisting some stressors that could damage the God-given wholeness that is hers.

I, on the other hand, meet the changes that come with travel into new territory. Dr. Hart, though, alludes that "change demands adjustment, and adjustment causes adrenaline arousal.

Our complex lives, with the many demands for change that confront us so frequently, can significantly increase our susceptibility to stress damage."[3] While seeing the world, meeting new people and experiencing the anointing that advances God's Kingdom is exciting to me, all of the stress that goes with this sort of life, especially today, takes its toll. However, that does not mean I do not like the adrenaline rush that goes with stress. After a couple of weeks at home, I find myself looking for my next assignment.

Many people never identify their boundaries, nor do they learn how to choose to remain inside the bounds that protect their emotions so they can live in joy. Many people like the "rush of change," while all along the change is damaging their quality of life. Dr. Hart continues by saying, "I have known quite a few people who have died from heart attacks. And most of these people enjoyed up to the last minute the process that led to the destruction of their cardiovascular systems. Remember, adrenal arousal is seldom unpleasant; it invigorates and excites while it wears our systems down."[4]

That may be true of me. The call that is on my life causes me to carry the burden of God's heart for the nations of the earth, even if down deep I know my health might be better if I did not continually process so many changes.

Why Stress and Anxiety Cause Illness

Our bodies do strange things when we hear a state of alarm or experience an emergency. Adrenaline is released like a river flowing into our physiological system. This disrupts normal functioning and produces a heightened state of arousal. We feel our hearts racing. Our digestion begins to react, and many hormones are released into the bloodstream to prepare us for what we must face. Life as we know it at that moment

171

changes. Every time this occurs, our ability to fight again is weakened. Eventually, this can cause our cells to rebel. This damages tissues, irritates our stomach and can result in ulcers.

I am not a big sleeper, so I have had to learn the consequential relationship between stress, high adrenal levels, lack of sleep and lack of recovery. Sleep is a natural restorer. God works while we sleep. God can speak to us through dreams and night visions. Satan loves to rob us of these moments. Therefore, we must break every pattern of the "night robber" if we are to move in simple faith and restoration. Sleep refreshes and rebuilds our hormonal levels.

If, through our anxious thoughts, this pattern of restorative sleep never forms, we seek after something through the day to help us find relief. Because we awaken tired and fall into fatigue early in the day, many of us find ourselves addicted to alcohol, cigarettes and food. A spirit of infirmity then attaches to our souls, affects our bodies and weakens us. This results in our inability to stand and fight.

If we are anxious, the blood carries anxious thoughts throughout our body. Every organ we have is affected. Our *brains* hurt. We have headaches. We panic and flow in anxiety. Our thoughts race, and we become indecisive or presumptive in our decision making. *Our hearts do not beat properly. We get out of sync with God's heartbeat.* Our blood pressure goes high. However, when we stand up to fight, it drops low. The roller-coaster ride is almost unbearable. We feel dizzy, light-headed, heavy, sleepy and hyped up, all at once. Stress and anxiety create acid stomach and heartburn in us. Then there is that diagnosis of fibromyalgia. Our necks ache, and our shoulders are filled with pain. Our joints feel as though they are on fire. We sweat, we have skin breakouts; we are cold one moment, hot another. Finally, we feel as though we cannot breathe. Then comes an asthma diagnosis. We have what is called a hyperventilation syndrome and live with shortness of breath.

Add to all that our emotions. We experience feelings of fear that impending doom is just around every corner. We lose the ability to sit and listen for very long. We squirm and create new anxious songs with our foot tapping and pacing. We sweat. We live with fatigue and lack of energy. We gain or lose weight. Irritability and anger overtake us. Note that the one caution Paul gives the church in Ephesus is that anger can cause us to become demonized (see Ephesians 4:26–27).

All of this depletes our immune system, and we lose the ability to fight off disease and infection. What was designed to fight off all the intruders in our body tissues has been defeated. Then we suffer pain. Pain is a result of our system giving way to a brain depleted of the body's natural morphine, endorphins.

Oh, My Aching Head!

I call this terrible state a chronic condition of lack of rest— better known as violation of God's Sabbath plan. Pam explained about Sabbath rest in an earlier chapter, but let me just give you my thoughts after I explain my plight.

Through the trauma of my early life, which I explained in a preceding chapter, I became asthmatic. I was prone to bronchial asthma. Every allergy there was, I seemed to have. I was known at times to go into anaphylactic shock if I ate certain things. When you are allergic to something, your tissues react. Something harmless to others becomes poisonous to you. And known toxins such as poison oak and sumac could simply be in the air and cause your eyes to swell.

I was hypersensitive like that, and this all continued into my adult life. Pam and I married early, so bless her, she coped. When I was in distress, she would help soothe me. We still laugh over the time that Pam, at nineteen, had her wisdom teeth and seven supernumerary teeth removed. This ordeal so distressed me that *I* came down with a severe migraine and took the pain pills she had from her oral surgery. Then she, with gauze-packed mouth, had to take me to the emergency room to get even more help.

Migraines and cluster headaches became a way of life for me. Sometimes the pain was debilitating. As I said earlier, I really did not have the normal capacity built within me to overcome or the adrenal health to resist. Migraines led to blood pressure problems. These led to severe intestinal and digestion issues. Let me summarize by saying I was a *mess* physically. Before long I was on blood pressure, digestion and headache medication. My prescribed pain medicine became candy. I knew that this was not God's way of life for me. However, I had to manage the complexities of my life somehow.

I loved the Lord. However, when a person loves the Lord but does not fully know His grace and love, Bible reading and prayer can become a duty. I was trying to manage my pain and anxious activities myself, and my daily Bible reading and prayer life added just one more hour of stress. I was constantly thinking, *I have to get this done so I can get focused for the day.*

On top of my daily life of stress, I dealt with the high-energy requirements of a demanding job. One night while working late at the office, I found myself on my knees under my desk. I heard myself asking the Lord, "Please, Lord, You have to give me a plan to move forward!"

Jonah lived an anxious life because he resisted carrying the burden that the Lord assigned him. However, there was a way of escape. Jonah 2:2 says, "I cried out to the LORD because of my affliction, and He answered me." And David said in Psalm 120:1, "In my distress I cried to the LORD, and He heard me." I cried out to the Lord for a way of escape, too. I knew that there was a Greater Spirit in me than in the world—I had been introduced to the Holy Spirit. But God! I knew He could help me, and that all things work together for good.

Because I am a burden bearer, what Jesus said about burdens became the key to my life: "My yoke is easy and My burden is light." (Matthew 11:30). I had to learn to bear burdens with Him and like Him. I had to learn the process of becoming more simple. For me, simplifying my life meant simplifying my *thinking* so that I could live *free from anxiety* and learn to *walk in the Spirit*.

Let me encourage you not to get frustrated if your health is a mess, like mine was, and your life is anxiety-filled and complex. There *is* a way of escape for you into simplicity. I have found that faith provides the right framework. Like me, your mind can shift and your spirit can be renewed. In my next chapter, I will provide some concrete examples of how you can simplify your thinking to live free from anxiety and learn to walk in His Spirit. All these things will work together for your good!

12

Simplicity Can Be a Reality

Certain events in the earth have occurred in the last seven-year cycle (starting in September 2001 and coinciding with but not determined by 9/11) that have created unstoppable motions of change, both in the world and in the Kingdom of God. The kingdom of darkness takes advantage of the structures of the world to work evil into the fabric of society. However, sinister darkness must give way to the Kingdom of God, which is advancing with new strength. God is releasing His supernatural power on His people and creating a unique anointing that will break the yokes of bondage in the earth. We are under the impulsion or driving force of a King who wants to see these changes manifest in a harvest such as has never been seen since the onset of the history of mankind.

We must gain momentum now. As we learn to move in our proper spheres of authority in the earthen realm, we will harness God's power and then release that power. The season ahead will be a transforming time for God's people. Once we are transformed, we will see cities, regions and nations changed. With great enthusiasm, we will enter harvest fields that are ripe. It is important not to let carnal impulses guide us during this time.

This sounds exciting, but at first glance, it can appear the opposite of simplicity. Thoughts of the future create anxiety in many. Fear instead of faith rises up in many of us when we look at the world today and then think another generation ahead. I would love to say that I always walk in simplicity on a daily basis, and that I never experience anxiety. I would love to say that I am always filled with faith. However, I can only say that on a daily basis, I consistently seek a Holy God to help me through each day.

In a world filled with crisis, I find that I must also resist the power of the world's complex, faith-robbing strategies on a daily basis. Therefore, as you read through this chapter, let me share some things I have learned (and relearned) as I pick up my cross daily and follow the One in whom I have chosen to put my trust as changes abound. In the midst of the stressful, day-to-day changes going on in the world, here are some points that will help you keep things simple as you process your daily life:

1. Start the day with one thought from the Lord and rehearse that simple thought before Him all day. If you embrace one thought at the beginning of each day and build on that thought, you will find your focus and faith work together to produce creative breakthrough.
2. Be a good listener. Listening is a priceless skill that can cause you to make every turn in life correctly. Listening well can simplify your life.
3. Be thankful for what you have and look for ways to *give*. Thankfulness and a grateful heart turn bad into good. Sacrificial giving produces joy.

4. Do not allow your spiritual energy to diminish. Resist overly stressful conditions, which neutralize your spiritual passion. The enemy will attempt to overload your senses with difficult decisions and then convince you that you will make the wrong choices. His goal is to freeze your progress.

5. Know your sphere of authority and where it fits in the authority structure of your field and workplace. Also, be aware of the accountability structure that exists within the field where you operate.

6. Tear down old strongholds from the past season of your life. Change begins with your thinking, so unclutter your thought processes to become more effective and efficient.

7. When questions are posed, embrace critical thinking.

8. Let your situations and circumstances unlock your creative genius.

9. Do not be afraid of the supernatural dimension that surrounds you. Walk under heaven's window.

10. Do not become frustrated when the old structures war against future prosperity.

11. Receive the *new* when you sense a release from heaven's storage vats. The *new way* will prevail and become established for the next season of your life.

12. Choose pauses and move in divine rests. Take your Sabbaths and enter your dominion rests.

Everything Is Changing

Just when I thought I was on my way to enjoying peace and feeling settled, God initiated the next call from heaven into our lives. My call was to work in China and the former Soviet bloc countries. Pam knew she was to begin her real career of extending our inheritance to another generation—having babies! The former, my call, was and is much less stressful than Pam's. With each child, I found new, uncovered anxiety realms inside me. Each pregnancy was eventful and filled with faith challenges. Yet each child has brought out the best in me—after I uncovered other layers of self and unbelief that needed sanctification. Now our kids are having kids, and I continue to change with each new arrival.

Everything around us is changing. Our children range from seventeen to forty. Our grandkids range from in the gestation stage to seventeen. The moral and social values in the world have changed drastically since we raised our first four children. How our last two children process the world is totally different from the first four's approach. The world's pressures and the influence from peers are more demanding now than they used to be. In order for our grandchildren to receive the inheritance of the Lord developed in my grandmother, our mothers and us, they, too, will have to develop faith. They must learn to develop thought processes built upon an absolute system that includes God's Law and embraces the grace His Son came to offer. Without this, they will find themselves stressed by the complexity of the world.

We will not entirely avoid situations that produce great amounts of stress in our lives. Some of us can make choices about areas such as jobs and geographical locations that alleviate some conflict for us. However, not all of us have the luxury of living away from all the confused noise of the world. So to live in harmony with our environment, we all must know and hold on to our values to remain simple in a complex, changing society. God intended us to live peacefully. His goal is for us to cultivate and multiply in the place He assigns us. He means for us to be efficient in what we do, maximizing time and space. His ultimate goal for us is to live in harmony with Him and with those who enter our lives and spheres.

Different Times—Different Thinking

When my book *The Future War of the Church* was first written and released (Regal Books, 2001), before the tragedy of 9/11, it urged the Church to alter its thinking about the war ahead. After 9/11, the book was easier to understand because times had changed. The conflict that once was imminent had become a reality. Concepts that I wrote about in those pages had transitioned from future to present. The book is about a seven-year war period that God's covenant people would go through that would prepare us for the world ahead and propel us into God's Kingdom plan. Actually, I believe God showed me this in advance so I could pray that we would all embrace the changes ahead. This book is now a history book of a season that changed the course of the world and the Church.

I thought everyone in Christendom would want to read the book when it came out. In January 2001, I began to promote the book by saying that the Lord had shown me that we would be in war in our nation by September 18. I thought this would excite everyone. However, it created great conflict, controversy and even much criticism from those who could not believe I would say such a thing. This conflict threw me into a level of stress beyond the normal level I already experience being a prophet. Because I could foresee some things that were going to happen, I began to carry a weighty burden for the Body of Christ.

As I saw the resistance the Body had to change, the weight of my burden grew each day. My anxiety level increased. I was traveling nonstop, praying all night and seeing into an unusual

181

spiritual realm. The problem was that I had not allowed the faith necessary to carry this burden to develop in me. I could not find rest. My adrenal system became exhausted and, consequently, illness touched my body. I actually became allergic to anything that entered my body. This condition escalated into dangerous anaphylactic shocks. I also developed diverticulitis and diverticulosis. I was a mess.

The day before I was hospitalized, I took two calls. The first was from Cindy Jacobs, who told me how concerned she was for my health. I began working with Mike and Cindy Jacobs in 1991. She is one of my dearest longtime friends, and a spiritual sister. Not only is her prophetic gift known around the world, but I trust her spiritual insights and counsel.

Cindy told me, "I think there is something linked with your dad that you have not dealt with fully."

I thought I had fully dealt with everything regarding him, and I had even written a book called *Possessing Your Inheritance* (Regal Books, 1999) that reflected on those past portions of my life. However, I politely told Cindy, "I'll ask the Lord."

My brother, Keith, then called from church after he had finished teaching a class and said, "While I was teaching, the Lord impressed me to tell you that there was something in your life that you need to see that is still linked back with our daddy and his situation."

Feeling physically bad and emotionally irked, I said, "He was your dad, also. Why are you never sick?"

Keith responded quickly, "Because you had an emotional tie with him that I didn't have!"

Those words pierced my heart and mind. I got on my knees and asked the Lord if there was something He needed to say to me since I had heard the same thing from two witnesses.

He spoke very clearly, *Do not forget My Sabbath, and your health and wholeness will spring forth!*

I immediately remembered an occasion after church one Sunday, when we were having lunch with a very devoted Christian aunt. We had gone over to her home after attending her church. When my dad dropped by to see us on the way to another engagement, my aunt said to him, "G. W., I have not seen you in church in a couple of years."

My dad replied, "Some need to worship, others need to work and make money!"

My dad had made the choice to stop worshiping and pursue the world. His example had impacted me, but the Lord had placed His finger on a key to the restoration of my soul and my physical health.

God's Rest—a Necessary Choice

I realized that I had a stronghold to deal with (again). I had participated in *Shabbat* for eight years before we had children. I continued eighteen years after we started having children. However, in my quest to see change and move forward, I had become remiss in spending time with the Lord and entering into a time of rest. I needed to apply this Sabbath principle to my prayer life as well. I had to carry a burden without violating the rest of God.

As Pam explained in her earlier chapter on simplicity and the Sabbath, rest is important. The Bible teaches that we are in a battle, engaged in a struggle against powers and principalities . . . against dark forces of evil in the world. Warfare can be intense—a battlefield is not a restful place. We need to be always alert and always diligent. We need to press through. That can be tiring after a while! If you have grown weary of the battle, there is good news. God has prepared a time for you to rest. When the battle gets hard and the struggle seems unending, you must find rest. In Hebrews 4:1, 9–11 (NIV) we read,

> Therefore, since the promise of entering his rest still stands, let us be careful that none of you be found to have fallen short of it. . . .
> There remains, then, a Sabbath-rest for the people of God; for anyone who enters God's rest also rests from his own work, just as God did from his. Let us, therefore, make every effort to enter that rest.

In the midst of pressing through obstacles and pursuing your destiny, you must take time to stop and remember that God is good. You can taste and see His goodness, experience relief and be restored. Rest is part of God's will for you and me. He could have designed our bodies to be on the go 24/7, but He did not. God's plan was that we would take time to rest every day, and He designed our bodies to cease activity several hours a day for sleep. This is not wasted time—it is God's design. Achieving simplicity, whether in the spiritual or physical, is impossible without following God's design for rest.

I took archery in college. An archer depends on the strength of his bow, but if he keeps it strung all the time, the string loses strength. To keep a bow strong, it must be unstrung and given time to rest. That is how God designed you also. If you keep your body strung on high alert all the time, as I talked about earlier, then when you are ready to shoot, you will not have the tension or elasticity necessary to aim well and hit your target. Like an archer, you need to find times to unstring your bow, so to speak. If you constantly push yourself beyond God's boundaries for your life, you will be ineffective and also miss a blessing God ordained for you.

God designed rest to bless us on many levels. Rest brings physical refreshment. Rest brings physical healing. Rest brings mental creativity. Many times, when you are wrestling with a problem, you find the answer after a good night's sleep. Your mind thinks in some ways during sleep that it cannot while you are awake. Rest brings revelation from God. Much revelation comes in dreams. Therefore, when you rest or sleep, the Spirit of God communicates with you in new ways and gives you divine restoration in body, mind and spirit. God designed the blessing of rest as an oasis on your journey. If you take time to rest, you will be happier, stronger and more prosperous. Your life will be simpler as a result, and you will live longer.

How do we find rest? Most of us are a people who find no rest, and the Bible describes that as a curse. Writer Wayne Muller describes it this way:

> The more our life speeds up, the more we feel weary, overwhelmed and lost. Despite our good hearts and equally good intentions, our life and work rarely feel light, pleasant or healing. Instead, as it all piles endlessly upon itself, the whole experience of being alive begins to melt into one enormous obligation. It becomes the standard greeting everywhere: "I am so busy." We say this to one another with no small degree of pride, as if our exhaustion were a trophy. To be unavailable to our friends and family, to be unable to find time for the sunset (or even to know that the sun has set at all), to whiz through our obligations without time for a single mindful breath—this has become the model of a successful life.[1]

Sabbath rest is a time of rest that is *regularly repeated*, a time when you cease from normal work and experience physical, mental and emotional rest. During this time, pressures and responsibilities must be lifted, and you should be free to simply enjoy God's goodness. Rest is a gift given by God at creation. Rest was woven into the fabric of the universe. One of the first expressions of God's will ever given was to rest one day out of seven. Rest is so important to God that He included the weekly Sabbath in the Ten Commandments. To violate God's will for us to rest is the same as violating His commands not to kill, steal or commit adultery! By the time of the New Testament, however, the Pharisees had taken God's blessing of rest and turned it into a legalistic burden. They stood around with their clipboards, judging everyone to make sure they were observing Sabbath correctly. They complicated the Sabbath until it was more anxiety producing than restful.

In *Reordering Your Day* (Glory of Zion, 2006), I share how *Shabbat* is the heart of God's covenant plan. We enter in by faith and experience a day of material and spiritual delight, so the desires of our hearts are purified and we can feel the delight of His presence. *Shabbat* is a time to "be still and know" in order to triumph over our enemies. It is a time to let a new dimension of faith rise in our midst so we can praise God in every circumstance.

You will not find a legalistic list for observing the Sabbath in the Bible. It just says, "Do no regular work." The goal is to enjoy God and His blessings. The New Testament teaching on Sabbath is found in Colossians 2:16, which says not to let anyone *judge you* in regard to Sabbath. In other words, "Don't be legalistic in your observance of Sabbath. Don't judge each other on how you observe it!" The goal of the New Testament teaching is to restore Sabbath to its original purpose: *a blessing from God.*

Sabbath is not a legalistic thing. Times will come when you need to work on a Sabbath. The Word says that even on Sabbath, if your ox falls into a ditch, you need to pull it out (see Luke 14:5). You also need to help people in need, even on a Sabbath. That is why Jesus healed on the Sabbath. You will not go to hell if you work on a Sabbath. But if you continually miss your Sabbaths, you are missing a blessing—you lose your joy, you lose your creativity, you lose your strength.

Sabbath rest is the first kind of rest God instituted for us, but there is also a second kind of rest: *dominion rest*. Robert Heidler says, "Sabbath Rest is a *time* of rest, but Dominion Rest is a *place* of rest." I had been striving so hard to see the Body of Christ take dominion over the evil invading forces, that I was driven for dominion rest at the cost of Sabbath rest.

Dominion rest is your personal promised land—your inheritance. This type of rest may include an actual physical location. It may include your place of ministry. It is your call, your destiny in the earth. All of us have a destiny chosen by God—a call, a purpose to accomplish in the earthen realm. When you take dominion of your inheritance so the enemy can no longer oppress you and steal it away, you enter dominion rest.

In Genesis 2:15, when God put man in the Garden, one translation of the Hebrew literally says God "rested" them there. The Garden was their inheritance. God placed them there and gave them dominion. It was their place of rest—a place of security and peace where they were not in turmoil and not under attack. God still has a place of rest for His people. For Israel it was the Promised Land. When Israel was secure in its land, they were said to have "rest." God has a place of rest for you also. You enter dominion rest when you take dominion of your God-given inheritance.

To enter dominion rest, we must first war and work. The Bible says we must *strive* to enter dominion rest. You only enter dominion rest when your enemies have been defeated.

187

The enemy always tries to occupy your inheritance (just as the Canaanites occupied the Promised Land). But when you drive the enemy from your inheritance, you enter dominion rest. You must *battle* to possess your inheritance. In Psalm 95 God swore that the Israelites who turned back from the ⚹ Promised Land would never enter His "rest" because they were not willing to *fight* to take possession of it. They refused to take dominion of their inheritance, and so forfeited the right to it. They died wandering in the wilderness.

In one of his teachings on why we observe the Sabbath, Robert Heidler says we do so "because God commanded it!" He adds:

- Sabbath is an act of worship, a way of acknowledging His greatness as Creator.
- Sabbath is a picture of salvation. It is a time to rest from our works and receive His blessings as a gift.
- Sabbath is a picture of heaven and anticipates the day when we will rest from our works and enjoy Him forever.
- Sabbath is designed to restore us and give us strength for the battles ahead.
- God says, "One day in seven take a break from the things you do to earn." If we do this, we will take dominion.

When we are obedient to observe Sabbath rest and are diligent to fight for and enter into dominion rest, then simplicity can be a reality for us. As Pam and I have found out, a simpler life full of the blessing of God is always the result.

Simple and Focused

I love moving in the prophetic and being a burden bearer in the Kingdom of God. I hate being anxious. How can I accomplish God's call, yet remain free from the anxiety that such a call seems to produce? This is the balance I have sought to find since my midtwenties. Achieving this balance is one of the driving goals of my life.

For you and me, staying simple and focused when we are being used of the Lord can sometimes seem impossible. Yet that is what Jesus modeled for us. He took on the burden of mankind, but He never did anything that He did not see the Father doing. He stayed simple and focused so He could accomplish His call in the earth. That defines success to me— staying simple and focused, as Jesus did, to accomplish our call. To meet God, know Him and align our thinking with His has tremendous rewards. Then when we encounter the enemy, we will overcome his wiles, methods and devices. To withstand the enemy and reach the result the Father intends is the most rewarding thing life has to offer.

We may be tempted toward anxiety along the way. We may have to strain every nerve to stay focused. But if we do only what the Father wishes us to do in a given situation, we will reach the goal He has assigned us. The burden may seem heavy, but as I said before, Jesus told us His yoke is easy and His burden is light (see Matthew 11:30). And in the end, we will be able to shout, "Mission accomplished!"

Think of Jesus at Gethsemane. His assignment was mankind's redemption. He carried the stress of His burden and stayed with His call until He triumphed. His will had to align with the Father's, for my sake and yours. If He arose from His knees before He aligned Himself with the Father, we all would lose the war of dominion and eternity. If He stayed and overcame His anxious thoughts and human inclinations, a door to life and life abundant would open to all of us.

Jesus withstood the stress of the burden, becoming the example for all of us in the midst of a trial where the way of

189

escape was difficult. He did express a wish that the Father would relieve Him of the burden, yet He was constrained by love for His Father and for humankind. So He overcame stress, anxiety, fear and pain. He stayed on His knees until He could stand and journey down a path that would free mankind. He bought and paid for our freedom and wholeness. Jesus revealed to us the way of success through simply obeying.

May you and I simply obey, and experience as a result the best that God has allotted for us. Whether good or bad situations come into our path, our simple love for Him can give us the strength to finish every race and hear the words, "Well done, My good and faithful servant. You simply obeyed Me. You aligned your mind with Me and developed My mind. You will enter into a great peace!"

When we obey, His love will overpower us. Be expectant. Watch for His coming visitation in your life. We are a people on the move in a world that is constantly moving. God has ✔ chosen to advance His Kingdom through you and me. As we see a manifestation of His promises in our lifetime, we are moving from fellowship into war and from praise into jubilation. This is a time of transcending old thinking, old ways and old problems, and employing new thinking, new ways and new strategies to take back what the enemy has held in captivity.

Pam's first word in this book sums up one of the best and most effective strategies God has given us for this very time: *Simplify!*

Postscript

Some Final Thoughts on Simplicity

L ast year, when the Lord woke me up with the word *simplify* bouncing around in my head, I had no idea where that one word would lead. In the months immediately following that experience, our lives became more complicated than ever. In spite of all the new situations that created an atmosphere of clutter and chaos, the word *simplify* continued to ring in my mind and my spirit. I knew that God's timing in delivering that one word into my life was no coincidence. That knowledge led Chuck and me to accept God's assignment to write this book.

During the last week of March 2009, while I was reviewing completed chapters and preparing to write this final entry, our lives were once again interrupted with circumstances beyond our control. On a Wednesday night just before bedtime, I started experiencing severe abdominal pains. I could not get comfortable and go to sleep, so I finally gave up. Like so many people in this age of information and technology,

I went to the computer to search for my symptoms on the Internet. (Do not judge me—I am not the only one who has done this!) By the time I finished searching, I had convinced myself that I was having a heart attack. In fact, the more symptoms I read, the more symptoms I had!

A little after midnight, I knew for certain that something beyond a miserable stomachache was the problem, so I woke my husband up.

"Chuck," I whispered, close to his sleeping head, "I hate to do this to you, but you're going to have to take me to the emergency room. I think I'm having a heart attack."

"What!" he said. He sat up quickly and threw his feet on the floor. "You can't be!"

"Well, something is going on that I've never felt before, and I'm not taking any chances," I replied.

For the next several minutes we scurried around, got dressed, woke Isaac, tried to wake Ethan (who sleeps like a bear in hibernation) and made a couple of phone calls. The trip to the hospital really was a "trip." Chuck is not the best driver in the world, and we were in the church van. He could not find the wipers, it was foggy outside and the headlights were not set to automatic, so we drove halfway in the dark. Chuck was not even wearing a seat belt. Add to that Chuck's constantly ringing cell phone, and you can imagine what a wild ride we had across town.

Thankfully, Chuck was right—I was not having a heart attack. Instead, I had acute pancreatitis. After two days in the hospital, a battery of tests and nothing to eat or drink, my doctor informed me that my gall bladder was the culprit and would have to come out. All I could think of was how thankful I had always been for excellent health, and now, here I was in the hospital with one of my organs turning traitor!

Sudden illness is one of the many circumstances that force us to evaluate our lives and reconsider our priorities. I believe what the Bible says in Romans 8:28: "And we know that all things work together for good to those who love God, to those who are the called according to His purpose." That includes even sickness. I also believe that God uses every circumstance, even the unpleasant ones, to teach, train and perfect His children. No experience is wasted in God's economy.

Many times when we find ourselves in situations beyond our control, we fret over what a waste of time some things really are. What purpose, we wonder, does sitting in a hospital room serve? What is the point in that broken pipe and a flooded house, that barren womb or that motorcycle accident? The truth is that the word *waste* is a concept we humans invented. Waste does not even occur in God's created world. In creation, everything has a purpose. In God's divine order, nothing that happens to us is wasted. Every situation has the potential to "work together for good."

As I type these words, I am sitting in my hospital room, waiting for tomorrow's surgery. I know that these past few days have been harder on my family than they have been on me. Certainly, it would have been easier for my husband, my children and my friends if I had continued being healthy and available. Obviously, it would also have been much more pleasant for me if that had been the case! Even so, my family has been forced to simplify their lives to accommodate the absence of wife, mother, occasional cook, dog wrangler and laundress. They are learning:

- to make simple or simpler;
- to reduce to basic essentials;
- to diminish in scope or complexity—streamline; and
- to make more intelligible—clarify.

Simplification is not about making life easier. It is about clearing away the cobwebs that obscure our vision. It is about choosing that "good part" and discarding the rest. It is about being free from the distractions that keep us from truly knowing and fellowshipping with our families, our friends and our God.

Notes

Chapter 1: Faith, Focus and Function

1. C. S. Lewis, *The Lion, The Witch and the Wardrobe* (New York: HarperCollins, 1994), 53.
2. *American Heritage College Dictionary*, 4th ed., s.v. "Simplify."
3. Harry Verploegh, ed., *Oswald Chambers: The Best from All His Books* (Nashville: Oliver-Nelson, 1989), 323.

Chapter 2: Understanding Simplicity

1. *American Heritage College Dictionary*, 4th ed., s.v. "Simple."
2. Ibid., s.v. "Circumspect."
3. Ibid., s.v. "Skill," "Gift," "Gifted."

Chapter 3: Fasting for Simplification

1. *American Heritage College Dictionary*, 4th ed., s.v. "Discipline."
2. See http://www.digitalhome.ca/content/view/3434/283.

Chapter 4: Simplicity and the Law of Love

1. See http://johnkellerupdate.blogspot.com.
2. See http://www.webmd.com/balance/guide/20070201/multitasking-hurts-learning.
3. *American Heritage College Dictionary*, 4th ed., s.v. "Stress."

Chapter 5: Simplicity, Sabbath and Refreshing

1. Robert Heidler, *The Messianic Church Arising! Restoring the Church to Our Covenant Roots* (Denton, Tex.: Glory of Zion International Ministries, 2006), 87.
2. Ibid.
3. Ibid., 88.
4. Fred Van Dyke et. al., *Redeeming Creation: The Biblical Basis for Environmental Stewardship* (Downer's Grove, Ill.: InterVarsity Press, 1996), 67–68.
5. Heidler, *Messianic Church Arising*, 87.
6. Ibid., 90.
7. Ibid., 93–94.
8. Van Dyke et. al., *Redeeming Creation*, 36–37.
9. Heidler, *Messianic Church Arising*, 94.

Chapter 6: Money, Possessions and Simplicity

1. *American Heritage College Dictionary*, s.v. "Mammon."
2. W. E. Vine, *Vine's Expository Dictionary of New Testament Words* (Iowa Falls, Iowa: Riverside Book and Bible House, 1952), s.v. "Godliness," "Contentment."
3. *American Heritage*, s.v. "Presume," "Presumption."
4. See http://www.medicinenet.com, March 29, 2004.

Chapter 7: Practicing Simplicity

1. See http://www.quotationspage.com/quotes/E. F. Schumacher.
2. See http://www.quotationvault.com/author/D. H. Mondfleur.
3. See http://www.catalogchoice.org.

Chapter 8: Simplicity or Anxiety?

1. Chuck D. Pierce and Rebecca Wagner Sytsema, *When God Speaks* (Ventura, Calif.: Regal Books, 2005), 70–71. Hamon quote from Jane Hamon, *Dreams and Visions* (Ventura, Calif.: Regal Books, 2000), 22–24.
2. Jonathan Davidson and Henry Dreher, *The Anxiety Book* (New York: Riverhead Books, 2003), 61.
3. Ibid., 21.

Chapter 10: Stress Can Work for You

1. Victor Pease, *Anxiety into Energy* (New York: Hawthorn/Dutton, 1981), 21.

2. Dr. Archibald D. Hart, *The Hidden Link Between Adrenaline and Stress* (Waco: Word Books, 1986), 20, 24–25.

Chapter 11: Faith: The Right Framework

1. Joseph T. Hallinan, *Why We Make Mistakes: How We Look without Seeing, Forget Things in Seconds, and Are All Pretty Sure We Are Way Above Average* (New York: Broadway Books, 2009), 93.
2. Dr. Archibald D. Hart, *The Hidden Link Between Adrenaline and Stress* (Waco: Word Books, 1986), 67.
3. Ibid., 50.
4. Ibid., 51.

Chapter 12: Simplicity Can Be a Reality

1. Wayne Muller, "Whatever Happened to Sunday?", *USA Weekend*, April 2–4, 1999; article excerpted from Wayne Muller, *Sabbath: Remembering the Sacred Rhythm of Rest and Delight* (Bantam Books, 1999).

About the Authors

Dr. Charles D. "Chuck" and Pamela J. Pierce are ordained ministers and have been married since 1973. They have six children and seven grandchildren, all of whom live in the Denton, Texas, area.

Chuck serves as president of Glory of Zion International Ministries, Inc. and president of Global Spheres, Inc., both in Denton, and is widely known for his prophetic gifting. He also serves as Harvest Watchman for Global Harvest Ministries in Colorado Springs, Colorado.

Pam is known for the gifted way she communicates faith principles in practical, day-to-day life. She has coauthored the book *One Thing: How to Keep Your Faith in a World of Chaos* (Destiny Image, 2006) with her husband. As a master gardener, Pam is committed to imparting her love of creation and gardening to children of all ages.

Chuck's and Pam's life experiences will help you to experience a new reality with God.